# NEW INSTANT GUIDE TO BRIDGE

*New Instant Guide to Bridge* is designed as a quick reference book for every bridge player who wants to be sure of the best bid, lead or play. It includes what you need to know for opening bids, responses and rebids. There is also guidance on opening leads, declarer play and defence so that the reader will have all the basic essentials of good play within easy reach.

This new edition brings bidding methods up to date to accord with current standard practice and includes sections on hand evaluation and competitive bidding strategy.

## By HUGH KELSEY *in the Master Bridge Series*

KILLING DEFENCE AT BRIDGE
MORE KILLING DEFENCE AT BRIDGE
SHARPEN YOUR BRIDGE TECHNIQUE
LOGICAL BRIDGE PLAY
KELSEY ON SQUEEZE PLAY
ADVENTURES IN CARD PLAY (with Geza Ottlik)
BRIDGE ODDS FOR PRACTICAL PLAYERS (with Michael Glauert)

## By RON KLINGER *in the Master Bridge Series*

BASIC BRIDGE: *The Guide to Good Acol Bidding and Play*
BETTER BRIDGE WITH A BETTER MEMORY • BRIDGE IS FUN
THE POWER OF SHAPE • WHEN TO BID, WHEN TO PASS
*GUIDE TO BETTER CARD PLAY • PLAYING TO WIN AT BRIDGE
GUIDE TO BETTER ACOL BRIDGE • 20 GREAT CONVENTIONS FLIPPER
GUIDE TO BETTER DUPLICATE BRIDGE
BRIDGE CONVENTIONS, DEFENCES AND COUNTERMEASURES
100 WINNING BRIDGE TIPS • 50 MORE WINNING BRIDGE TIPS
100 WINNING DUPLICATE TIPS • ACOL BRIDGE MADE EASY
THE MODERN LOSING TRICK COUNT • PRACTICAL SLAM BIDDING
IMPROVE YOUR BRIDGE MEMORY
IMPROVE YOUR DECLARER PLAY AT NO-TRUMPS
IMPROVE YOUR OPENING LEADS • ACOL BRIDGE FLIPPER
RON KLINGER'S MASTER CLASS • 5-CARD MAJOR STAYMAN
RON KLINGER ANSWERS YOUR BRIDGE QUERIES
THE LAW OF TOTAL TRICKS FLIPPER • BASIC ACOL BRIDGE FLIPPER
DUPLICATE BRIDGE FLIPPER • MODERN LOSING TRICK COUNT FLIPPER
MEMORY AIDS & USEFUL RULES FLIPPER
BID BETTER, MUCH BETTER AFTER OPENING 1 NO-TRUMP
5-CARD MAJORS • 5-CARD MAJORS FLIPPER
TO WIN AT BRIDGE • †RIGHT THROUGH THE PACK AGAIN
BETTER BALANCED BIDDING (with David Jackson)
DEADLY DEFENCE (with Wladyslaw Izdebski and Roman Krzemien)
THE DEADLY DEFENCE QUIZ BOOK
(with Wladyslaw Izdebski and Roman Krzemien)

*Winner of the 1991 Book of the Year Award of the
American Bridge Teachers' Association
†Winner of the 2009 International Bridge Association Book of the Year Award

# NEW INSTANT GUIDE TO BRIDGE

Hugh Kelsey &
Ron Klinger

Weidenfeld & Nicolson
IN ASSOCIATION WITH
PETER CRAWLEY

Fifth revised edition published in Great Britain 2011
Second impression 2012
in association with Peter Crawley
by Weidenfeld & Nicolson
a division of the Orion Publishing Group Ltd
Orion House, 5 Upper St Martin's Lane, London, WC2H 9EA

an Hachette UK Company

A catalogue record for this book is available from the British Library

ISBN: 978 0 297 86457 8

Printed in Great Britain by Clays Ltd, St Ives plc

The Orion Publishing Group's policy is to use papers that are natural,
renewable and recyclable products and made from wood grown in sustainable
forests. The logging and manufacturing processes are expected to conform to
the environmental regulations of the country of origin.

www.orionbooks.co.uk

# Contents

## Scoring table

*Below the line*

**Trick score**

For each trick over six

| bid and made: | UNDOUBLED | DOUBLED | REDOUBLED |
|---|---|---|---|
| In Clubs or Diamonds | 20 | 40 | 80 |
| In Hearts of Spades | 30 | 60 | 120 |
| In No-trumps (first trick) | 40 | 80 | 160 |
| (each subsequent trick) | 30 | 60 | 120 |

The first side to score 100 points below the line wins a game and is said to be vulnerable. Both sides start from scratch for the next game. The first side to win two games wins the rubber.

*Above the line*

**Bonuses**

**For honours in one hand**

All five trump honours, or four aces at no-trumps: 150

Four trump honours: 100

| **For bidding and making a slam** | NOT VULNERABLE | VULNERABLE |
|---|---|---|
| Small slam (12 tricks) | 500 | 750 |
| Grand slam (13 tricks) | 1000 | 1500 |

| **For winning the rubber** | **Unfinished rubber** |
|---|---|
| In two games: 750 | One game in unfinished rubber: 300 |
| In three games: 500 | A part-score in unfinished game: 100 |

For making any doubled contract: 50

For making any redoubled contract: 100

| **For each overtrick made:** | UNDOUBLED | DOUBLED | REDOUBLED |
|---|---|---|---|
| Not vulnerable | Trick value | 100 | 200 |
| Vulnerable | Trick value | 200 | 400 |

**Undertricks** (penalties scored by defenders if declarer falls short of contract)

| *Not vulnerable* | | | | | *Vulnerable* | | | |
|---|---|---|---|---|---|---|---|---|
| Down | 1 | 2 | 3 | Then | 1 | 2 | Then |
| Undoubled | 50 | 100 | 150 | 50 each | 100 | 200 | 100 each |
| Doubled | 100 | 300 | 500 | 300 each | 200 | 500 | 300 each |
| Redoubled | 200 | 600 | 1000 | 600 each | 400 | 1000 | 600 each |

# Introduction

When the late Hugh Kelsey first wrote *Instant Guide to Bridge*, he had this to say, 'This little book does not aim to teach bridge to the absolute beginner. It is designed as a reference text for those who have learned the mechanics of the game but are still uncertain of finding the right bid or play in the situations that constantly recur at the bridge table.

Do not attempt to read through from cover to cover, for a surfeit of condensed information can lead only to mental indigestion. The right way to use the book is to refer to the relevant section as you encounter a problem. Wrestle with each difficulty as it arises and you will have less trouble with similar situations in the future.

The recommendations in the bidding sections are tied to the Acol system, which is by far the most popular method in use in Britain today. If you play Acol you can be sure of finding a partner who speaks the same language in any corner of the country.

In a book of this size the amount of space devoted to the play of the cards is necessarily limited. Nevertheless, the reader who masters the sections on play and defence will have the basic elements of good play at his fingertips.'

Hugh updated some material in the 1990 edition and introduced a number of conventions such as transfer bids, negative doubles and Roman Key Card Blackwood. In the 1994 edition, the scoring table was revised to take account of important changes introduced by the International Laws of Contract Bridge 1993.

*New Instant Guide To Bridge* follows Hugh's style and aims to bring the bidding content into line with modern standard Acol. Popular new conventions are included, as well as new wrinkles on accepted methods. A word about notation: '+' means 'or more', so '13+ points' = '13 points or more'. Bids in brackets, such as (3♠) are bids made by the opponents.

*Ron Klinger, 2003*

# The point count

**Ace = 4    King = 3    Queen = 2    Jack = 1**

The point count is a reliable guide to the trick-taking capacity of a hand at no-trumps, but it is less accurate for suit contracts where shape and controls play a large part.

Do not apply the point count too rigidly. Make allowance for a long suit by shading the requirements for an opening bid. Support partner more readily when you have four trumps and a singleton or a void. Let the possession of good intermediate cards such as tens, nines and eights influence your decisions.

Having learned to make automatic adjustments of this sort, experienced players do not consciously add on points for distribution. When bridge players talk about points they mean high-card points, as does any reference to points in this book.

## Point count targets

There are 40 points in the pack and therefore 10 in an average hand. Add the points in your hand to the points indicated by your partner's bidding to arrive at the trick target for the combined hands.

WITH A TOTAL OF:    YOU CAN EXPECT TO MAKE:

| | |
|---|---|
| **20-24** | A part-score (7-9 tricks) |
| **25-27** | Game in 3NT (9 tricks) or game in 4♡ or 4♠ (10 tricks) |
| **28-29** | Game in 5♣ or 5♢ (11 tricks) |
| **30-32** | A possible small slam in a suit (12 tricks), depending on shape and controls |
| **33-36** | Small slam in a suit or in 6NT (12 tricks) |
| **37-40** | A grand slam (all 13 tricks) |

8

# The losing trick count (LTC)

The LTC is a superior method for estimating the partnership's trick potential when a good trump fit is held (at least eight trumps between you) or when one of the partners has a long, powerful suit which will be the trump suit.

(A) LTC formula when you have ruffing potential:

**1. Count**   *Your losers*
**2. Add**   *Partner's losers*
**3. Deduct**   *This total from 24*

The answer is the number of tricks the partnership will win in the agreed trump suit *most of the time*, assuming suits break normally and half of your finesses work.

*Your losers:*

Void = 0 losers
Singleton ace = 0 losers, other singletons = 1 loser.
Doubleton A-K = 0 losers, A-x or K-x = 1, other doubletons = 2.
3-card and longer suits: Consider only the top three cards. Count the A, K or Q as a winner, J or lower as losers. Thus: A-K-Q = 0 losers, suits headed by A-K-x, A-Q-x, K-Q-x = 1.
Suits headed by A-x-x, or K-x-x = 2. J-x-x or worse = 3.
Suit headed by the queen: Count as two losers if the suit has been bid by partner or is headed by Q-J or Q-10. Otherwise, count a Q-high suit as 2½ losers.

Examples:

| ♠ A K 7 2 = 1 | ♠ A K 7 2 = 1 | ♠ A K 7 2 = 1 |
| ♡ 9 8 4  = 3 | ♡ K 8 4  = 2 | ♡ K 8 4  = 2 |
| ◇ K Q 7 5 = 1 | ◇ K Q 7 5 = 1 | ◇ K Q 7 5 = 1 |
| ♣ J 2  = 2 | ♣ J 2  = 2 | ♣ A 2  = 1 |
| 13 points, 7 losers | 16 points, 6 losers | 19 points, 5 losers |

*As the points increase, the losers decrease.*

| ♠ A J 7  = 2 | ♠ A J  = 1 | ♠ A J  = 1 |
| ♡ K 8 4 3 2 = 2 | ♡ K 8 4 3 2 = 2 | ♡ K 8 6 4 3 2 = 2 |
| ◇ K Q 7 5  = 1 | ◇ K Q 7 5 4 = 1 | ◇ K Q 7 5 4  = 1 |
| ♣ 6  = 1 | ♣ 6  = 1 | ♣ - - -  = 0 |
| 13 points, 6 losers | 13 points, 5 losers | 13 points, 4 losers |

*The more shapely the hand, the fewer the losers.*

9

*Partner's losers:*

A minimum opening hand around 13-15 points tends to have 7 losers. There are 40 points in the pack and 13 tricks. Each trick is therefore valued at about 3 points. Each 3 points above 15 = one extra trick and so one less loser. Each 3 points below 13 = one trick less and one more loser.

| | | | |
|---|---|---|---|
| 13-15 = 7 losers | 16-18 = 6 | 19-21 = 5 | 22-24 = 4 |

| | | | |
|---|---|---|---|
| 13-15 = 7 losers | 10-12 = 8 | 7-9 = 9 | 4-6 = 10 |

These are reasonable working approximations for these point ranges when the hand is balanced. The wilder the shape, the fewer the losers for the same point count. Here is an example:

| | W | E | |
|---|---|---|---|
| ♠ A K Q 7 4 | | | ♠ 8 3 |
| ♡ K Q 8 4 3 | 1♠ | 2♡ | ♡ A 9 6 5 2 |
| ◇ K 5 | 4NT | 5♡ | ◇ A J 7 3 |
| ♣ 6 | 6♡ | No | ♣ J 4 |

West has 3 losers. On hearing 2♡, 10+ points, West places East with 8 losers or fewer. 3 + 8 = 11. 24 – 11 = 13, and so West sees potential for 7♡. West checks on aces and settles for 6♡ when an ace is missing. Opposite 3 aces, West would bid 7♡.

**(B) LTC formula when one partner has no ruffing potential:**
**1. Count** *The losers in the hand with the long, strong suit*
**2. Deduct** *Expected winners in the other hand*
**3. Deduct** *This total from 13*
The answer is the number of tricks you are likely to win.
Probable winners in partner's hand:

| | | | |
|---|---|---|---|
| 0-5 points: 0-1 | 6-9 points: 2 | 10-12 points: 3 | 13-15: 4 |

| | W | E | |
|---|---|---|---|
| ♠ A K Q J 7 4 | | | ♠ 8 5 2 |
| ♡ A 9 4 | 1♠ | 1NT | ♡ 7 6 3 2 |
| ◇ A 5 | 4♠ | No | ◇ K Q 3 |
| ♣ 6 3 | | | ♣ J 4 2 |

As East is unlikely to have ruffing value, West uses method (B). West has 5 losers. With 6-9 points East is likely to have 2 tricks. 5 losers – 2 tricks = 3 losers. 13 cards – 3 losers = 10 tricks expected. Therefore West jumps to 4♠.

# When to open the bidding

An opening bid normally indicates a hand that is better than average. Be guided by the following table.

| POINTS | ACTION | NOTES |
|---|---|---|
| **0-9** | Pass | For exceptions, see page 55 (pre-empts) |
| **10** | Generally pass | But open with a good 6+ suit or two 5-card suits |
| **11** | Generally pass | But open with a 6+ suit or a 5-4 pattern |
| **12** | a) Pass | With a bare 12 and a 4-3-3-3 pattern |
| | b) Open | With extra values, such as a 5-card suit, a couple of tens or not a 4-3-3-3 hand |
| **13 or more** | Always open | You cannot afford to pass with 13 points. If partner has 12 or more, the combined values give you a good chance for game. |

Other guidelines for opening:

*The Rule of 20*: Add your HCP to the number of cards in your two longest suits. If the total is 20 or more, open. (A rough guide.)

*Rule of 22:* Add your HCP, your two longest suits, quick tricks (QT) and adjustments. If the total is 22 or more, open the bidding.
*Quick tricks:* A-K = 2, A-Q = 1½, A = 1, K-Q = 1, K-x = ½
*Adjustments:* Add ½ for Q in A-K-Q, the J in a suit with two higher honours, J-10 in a suit with one higher honour. Deduct 1 for K, Q or J singleton or Q-J doubleton. Deduct ½ for A singleton or for A, K, Q or J in a doubleton holding. With 8 or 9 cards in the two longest suits, add ½ for a singleton or void; with 10 or 11 cards in the two longest suits, add ½ for a void.
Examples of the Rule of 22:
♠: A J 8 5 4   ♡: K Q 6 3 2   ◇: 8 4   ♣: 7   Total: 22. Open.
This hand has 10 HCP, 10 in two longest suits and 2 quick tricks.
♠: A 8 5 4 2   ♡: J 7 6 3 2   ◇: K Q   ♣: 7   Total: 21. Pass.
Deducting ½ each for the K and Q in the doubleton suit.
♠: A Q 8 5 4 3   ♡: 5 2   ◇: A 8 4 2   ♣: 7   Total: 22½. Open.

11

## Choice of suit

**With unequal length in your suits, open in the longer suit.**

♠: A K J 5  ♥: 5 2  ◇: Q 8 6 4 2  ♣: J 3  Open 1◇
♠: A K Q 9 4  ♥: A Q 10 6 5 2  ◇: 7  ♣: 8  Open 1♥
♠: A K 5 3  ♥: - - -  ◇: A J 7 3  ♣: J 6 4 3 2  Open 1♣

**With 6-6 or 5-5 patterns, open in the higher ranking suit.**

♠: J 9 8 6 5  ♥: 2  ◇: A K Q 4 2  ♣: Q 3  Open 1♠
♠: - - -  ♥: K J 9 4 3 2  ◇: A Q 7 6 3 2  ♣: 4  Open 1♥
♠: A K 8 5 3  ♥: 9  ◇: J 8  ♣: A J 6 5 2  Open 1♠

With 5-5 in spades – clubs, it would be efficient to open 1♣
and rebid in spades cheaply if the opponents are silent. That is
the problem. If you open 1♣ and the opponents bid briskly in a
red suit, it may be too high for you to introduce the spades.
Better to open 1♠ and perhaps lose the clubs than *vice versa*.

### With a 4-3-3-3 hand outside the no-trump ranges

Bid the 4-card suit.

### With a 4-4-3-2 hand outside the no-trump ranges

With 4-4 in the majors, always open 1♥:
♠: K Q 9 4  ♥: J 7 5 2  ◇: A Q  ♣: K J 3  Open 1♥
This allow partner to bid spades cheaply.
With 4-4 in the minors, open the stronger suit. If the opponents
win the contract, you have guided partner to the better lead.
♠: 8 7 2  ♥: A J  ◇: A K J 3  ♣: K 7 4 3  Open 1◇
With a major and a minor, open the major:
♠: K J 3  ♥: A J 6 2  ◇: A Q  ♣: K 9 8 4  Open 1♥

### With a 4-4-4-1 pattern

With a red singleton, open a suit below the singleton:
♠: Q J 8 5  ♥: 6  ◇: A Q 6 3  ♣: K 7 5 4  Open 1◇
With the minors reversed, you would open 1♣, the stronger suit.
With a black singleton, open the middle suit:
♠: Q J 8 5  ♥: A J 7 5  ◇: K Q J 3  ♣: 4  Open 1♥
♠: 7  ♥: K 8 7 4  ◇: K 6 4 3  ♣: A K J 4  Open 1◇

**Biddable suits**

It is attractive to have honours in a bid suit but it is not required. Any 4-card suit is biddable and any 5-card suit is rebiddable (that is, you may rebid such a suit if no better option exists; it does not suggest it is attractive to repeat a 5-card suit).

## Opening in third seat

With 13 HCP or more make your normal opening bid. With fewer HCP, open only in a suit which you will be happy for partner to lead. As you are unlikely to win the auction if partner could not open and you are below 13 HCP, your opening will be useful as long as it indicates a sound lead for partner. Be prepared to make a light opening in third seat as long as you are bidding a 5-card suit headed by K-Q or better or a 4-card suit K-Q-10-x or better.

If the auction has gone No bid, No bid to you and you hold:

♠: 8 5   ♡: Q 8 7 4 3   ◇: K Q   ♣: A 6 4 2    No bid.
♠: 8 5   ♡: 8 6 3 2    ◇: K Q   ♣: A Q 9 4 3   Open 1♣
♠: A K J 2   ♡: J 7 6 4   ◇: Q 10 3   ♣: 5 3    Open 1♠
♠: K 8    ♡: Q 7 6 3   ◇: A J 6   ♣: Q 5 3 2    No bid
♠: 4 2   ♡: A K Q 2   ◇: 8 2   ♣: J 9 8 6 4    Open 1♡

If not prepared to open 1♡, pass. Do not open 1♣

♠: 8 7 4 2   ♡: K 8 5 2   ◇: 7 4   ♣: A K Q    Open 1♣

If you cannot bear to open 1♣ on the last hand, pass.

Having opened light in third seat, you are expected to pass partner's response. Opening in third seat and bidding again indicates a sound opening

## Opening in fourth seat

With 13 HCP or more, make the normal opening bid. If weaker, add your HCP and the number of spades held. If the total is 15 or more, open. If less than 15, pass it in. If your count is below 13, each side might have around 20 points. In that case, the side that owns the spade suit often wins the part-score battle.

If there have been three passes to you and you hold:

♠: 8 7   ♡: K J 6 3   ◇: 7 4   ♣: A K 6 4 3    Pass it in
♠: K J 6 3   ♡: 8 7   ◇: 7 4   ♣: A K 6 4 3    Open 1♣

## Opening bids on balanced hands

**A balanced hand** is one with no singleton or void and not more than one doubleton. There are three balanced patterns: 4-4-3-2, 5-3-3-2 and 4-3-3-3, in order of frequency. With such a hand, it is normal to open the bidding in no-trumps or, lacking support for partner's suit, to rebid in no-trumps at the first opportunity.

The 1NT opening in Acol is played as 12-14 points, which is the range preferred by the vast majority of players in Britain. Some use a strong 1NT opening (15-17) and others play a weak 1NT when not vulnerable and a strong 1NT if vulnerable. If playing the strong NT, deduct 3 points for the point ranges for responder's actions given later.

*Recommended:* Play the weak 1NT throughout but beware of opening 1NT in third seat on a bare 12 points, especially when vulnerable. 1NT is acceptable with 12 HCP and a 5-card suit or suits including 10s and 9s. After two passes to you, if you hold:

♠: 9 6    ♡: K J 10    ◇: A J 10    ♣: K 10 9 6 2    Open 1NT
♠: 7 5 2    ♡: A Q J 4    ◇: 9 7 4 3    ♣: K Q    Open 1♡

## Bidding table for balanced hands

Traditional Acol

| POINTS | OPENER'S ACTION IF NO TRUMP FIT HAS BEEN FOUND |
|---|---|
| 12-14 | Open 1NT |
| 15-16 | Open 1-in-a-suit and rebid 1NT over a suit response at the 1-level and 2NT after a response at the 2-level |
| 17-18 | Open 1-in-a-suit and rebid 2NT over a suit response at the 1-level. This 2NT rebid is not forcing. After a suit response at the 2-level, rebid 2NT (forcing). |
| 19 | Open 1-in-a-suit and rebid 3NT after a suit reply |
| 20-22 | Open 2NT |
| 23-24 | Open 2♣, rebid 2NT (see page 44) |
| 25-27 | Open 2♣, rebid 3NT (see also pages 47 and 49) |

Because the 2NT and 3NT rebids after a 1-level suit reply make game exploration awkward, many prefer these alternatives:

*Attractive alternative 1:* Open 2NT with 21-22 (count 20 with a 5-card suit as 21). After a suit response at the one-level, use the jump-rebid to 2NT with 19-20, forcing to game, and rebid 1NT with 15-18. Responder has methods to determine opener's count within the 15-18 range (see pages 36-37).

*Attractive alternative 2:* Open 2NT with 20-22. After a suit response at the one-level, rebid 1NT with 15-17 and 2NT with 18-19, forcing. Responder has methods to determine opener's count within the 15-17 range (see pages 36-37).

After a 2-level new suit response, taken as 10+ points or 8-9 points and a long suit, the 2NT rebid, showing 15+ points is forcing to game, since the partnership has 25+ points or the equivalent based on responder's long suit.

For the strong 1NT opening:

| POINTS | OPENER'S ACTION IF NO TRUMP FIT HAS BEEN FOUND |
|---|---|
| 12-14 | Open 1-in-a-suit. Rebid 1NT over a reply at the 1-level or 2NT over a new suit at the 2-level. |
| 15-17 | Open 1NT. |
| 18-19 | Open 1-in-a-suit and jump-rebid in no-trumps, 2NT (forcing to game) over a suit response at the 1-level and 3NT over a suit response at the 2-level. |
| 20-up | Same as for the weak 1NT opening (see opposite). |

## Responding to the 12-14 1NT with a balanced hand

With no long suit and no 4-card or longer major, simply add the points in your hand to 12-14 to determine whether you are in the part-score, game or slam zone.

| POINTS | RESPONSE | NOTES |
|---|---|---|
| 0-11 | Pass | Game is unlikely. |
| 12 | 2NT | Inviting 3NT. Opener bids 3NT with 13 or 14 points. |
| 13-18 | 3NT | Slam is unlikely with a maximum of 32. |
| 19-20 | 4NT | Inviting slam if opener has 13-14. |
| 21-up | 6NT / 7NT | Depending on the combined total. |

## Responding to the 12-14 1NT with a 6+ suit

| POINTS | RESPONSE | NOTES |
|---|---|---|
| 0-9 | a) Bid 2 in suit | With any suit except clubs. |
| | b) Pass | If the suit is clubs.* |
| | c) Bid 4♡ / 4♠ | With 7-9 points and a 7+ major. |
| 10-16 | a) Bid 4♡ / 4♠ | With 6+ in the major suit. |
| | b) Bid 3NT | With 6+ minor suit. If the count is minimum, the suit must be good. |
| 17-up | Bid 3 in suit | Follow with a slam try on the next round (see pages 24, 51). |

*If playing transfers it may be safer to transfer and play in 3♣ with 6+ clubs rather than stay in 1NT.

## Responding to the 12-14 1NT with an unbalanced or semi-balanced hand (no suit longer than five cards)

'Semi-balanced': the hand contains two or three doubletons. There are three semi-balanced patterns: 5-4-2-2, 6-3-2-2, 7-2-2-2. 'Unbalanced': the hand contains a void or a singleton.

| POINTS | RESPONSE | NOTES |
|---|---|---|
| 0-10 | a) Bid 2 in suit | With any 5-card suit except clubs. |
| | b) Pass | If the suit is clubs. |
| | c) Bid 2♣ | With length in both majors. See Stayman Convention opposite. |
| 11-12 | a) 2NT | With length in the minor suits. |
| | b) 2♣ | Stayman with one or both majors. |
| 13-17 | a) 3NT | With length in the minor suits. |
| | b) 3♡ or 3♠ | With a 5-card major. |
| | c) 2♣ | Stayman with a 4-card major or with both majors. |
| 18-up | a) 3-in-suit | With a 5-card suit and no 4-card major. You are looking for slam. Opener should support with 3-4 trumps, bid 3NT with a doubleton. |
| | b) 2♣ | Stayman with a 4-major. If no major fit, bid 5-card suit (forcing). |

## The Stayman convention

The bid of 2♣ in response to a 1NT opening is artificial, asking whether the opener has a 4-card major. If so, opener bids 2♡ or 2♠ to show the suit held. If holding both majors, bid 2♡. With no major suit, the response is 2♢ (artificial).

There are several versions of the Stayman convention. In the most popular one, known as non-forcing Stayman, the responder may be quite weak if the hand pattern is suitable. The convention is used to guide the partnership into the best game or slam contract or into a safer part-score than 1NT.

There are two types of weak hands on which the responder may use Stayman. The first is with 5-4 in the majors. For example, partner opens 1NT and you hold:

♠: K 10 5 3    ♡: J 10 8 4 3    ♢: 7    ♣: J 10 4

This hand looks as though it will play better in one of your suits. You could make a weakness take-out of 2♡ but partner may have four spades and only two hearts, in which case 2♠ will be better. The solution is to respond with a Stayman 2♣. If opener rebids 2♡ or 2♠ you will be happy to pass. If opener bids 2♢, denying a 4-card major, you continue with 2♡, which opener will pass.

♠: A 9 8 5 4    ♡: Q 10 6 5    ♢: 8 4    ♣: 6 2

Similarly on this hand you respond 2♣ rather than 2♠. If partner bids either major you will be content. If the rebid is 2♢, you convert to 2♠, which opener will pass.

The other type of weak hand suitable for Stayman is a three-suited hand with shortage in clubs:

♠: J 10 5 2    ♡: 9 8 6 5    ♢: K 9 7 5 3    ♣: - - -
♠: A 7 6    ♡: Q 5 4 2    ♢: 10 9 7 5 4    ♣: 8

On either of these hands a suit contract is likely to be an improvement on 1NT. Respond 2♣ and pass opener's rebid, whether it is 2♢, 2♡ or 2♠.

# The Stayman convention *continued*

Stayman is also used to locate a 4-4 major-suit fit on hands where the responder has the strength to invite or to insist on game or slam. In such cases responder will have 11 or more points facing a weak 1NT and at least one 4-card major suit.

♠: K J 6 4   ♡: K 5   ◇: A 9 4 3   ♣: 10 7 6

After partner's weak 1NT, use Stayman to probe for a spade fit. If partner rebids 2♠, invite game with a raise to 3♠. If the rebid is 2◇ or 2♡, continue with 2NT. This is still a game invitation and it also guarantees four spades, so that with four spades as well as four hearts, opener can now bid spades, 3♠ if minimum or 4♠ if maximum.

♠: Q 4 3   ♡: A J 9 4   ◇: 9 7   ♣: A K 4 2

This time you have enough to insist on game after a weak 1NT from partner. Again you should start with Stayman. If opener rebids 2♡, simply raise to 4♡. If the rebid is 2◇ or 2♠, continue with 3NT.

♠: Q 10 6 4   ♡: K Q 7 2   ◇: A Q 6 5   ♣: 2

Strong hands with both majors are ideal for the use of Stayman. If opener rebids in either major you can raise to game. If the rebid is 2◇, jump to 3NT.

♠: A 10 9 5   ♡: K Q J 4 2   ◇: 7   ♣: K 5 3

Here you are 5-4 in the majors. Start with Stayman 2♣ and raise a major-suit rebid to game. If the rebid is 2◇, jump to 3♡. A new suit at the 3-level by the Stayman bidder shows at least five cards and is forcing. Opener is asked to choose between 4♡ and 3NT.

When responder bids a minor suit after Stayman, this shows a strong hand with slam potential.

♠: K Q 7 5   ♡: A 5   ◇: A K J 6 4   ♣: Q 9

Start with 2♣ in response to 1NT. No matter what partner rebids, continue with 3◇ to show slam interest. You can always support spades at a later stage if appropriate.

18

# The Stayman convention *continued*

Should you use Stayman 2♣ with a 4-3-3-3 pattern where the 4-card suit is a major? Opinion is divided. Some favour staying with no-trumps, others argue that seeking the major fit will find the superior game more often.

|  |  |
|---|---|
| ♠ A K 4 | ♠ 8 5 2 |
| ♡ A 9 4 3 | ♡ K Q J 6 |
| ◇ J 10 7 | ◇ A K Q |
| ♣ 9 6 4 | ♣ 8 7 5 |

Here East is a hero to bid 1NT : 3NT since there are only nine tricks in hearts and you will make nine tricks in 3NT most of the time (if clubs are 4-3 or a club is not led).

|  |  |
|---|---|
| ♠ A K 4 | ♠ 8 5 2 |
| ♡ A 9 4 3 | ♡ K Q J 6 |
| ◇ J 10 7 4 | ◇ A K Q |
| ♣ 9 6 | ♣ 8 7 5 |

This time 4♡ is much better. A club lead will beat 3NT most of the time while there are should be no problem in 4♡.

In general, with a 4-3-3-3 opposite a 4-3-3-3, you are better off in no-trumps, but with a 4-3-3-3 opposite a 4-4-3-2, the major-suit game is often superior. The problem is that responder cannot tell whether opener is 4-4-3-2 or 4-3-3-3.* As a matter of odds, with four hearts opener is more likely to be 4-4-3-2: there are six such patterns, 4-4-2-3, 4-4-3-2, 2-4-4-3, 3-4-4-2, 2-4-3-4, 3-4-2-4, and only one 3-4-3-3 pattern. For a 2♠ reply to Stayman, opener has four 4-4-3-2 pattern (4-2-4-3, 4-3-4-2, 4-2-3-4, 4-3-2-4) and only one 4-3-3-3 pattern.

The counter argument is that 1NT : 2♣ may give the defenders useful information when no major suit fit exists. That may spell defeat for 3NT, which might make after 1NT : 3NT.

*Recommended:* Use Stayman 2♣ with a 4-card major even with a 4-3-3-3 pattern. Aim to play in the better contract.

---

*Bid Better, Much Better After Opening 1NT*, published by Weidenfeld & Nicolson / Peter Crawley, allows you to discover whether opener is 4-3-3-3.

## The Stayman convention *continued*

*Summary of responder's action on the next round*

| POINTS | WHEN OPENER REBIDS 2◇ OR THE WRONG MAJOR | WHEN OPENER REBIDS THE RIGHT MAJOR |
|---|---|---|
| 11-12 | Bid 2NT. | Raise to 3 in major. |
| 13-18 | a) Bid 3NT.<br>b) Bid 3♡ or 3♠ with a 5-card suit. | Raise to 4 in major.<br>Raise to 4 in major or make a slam try if maximum. |

With greater strength responder should make a slam try (or bid slam directly) whether a fit is found or not.

## Rebids by the 1NT opener

The following table indicates the action to be taken by the opener after various sequences that start with a bid of 1NT.

| ON THE SEQUENCE: | OPENER SHOULD: |
|---|---|
| 1NT : 2◇ / 2♡ / 2♠ | Pass. |
| 1NT : 2♣ | a) Bid a 4-card major.<br>b) Bid 2◇ with no 4-card major. |
| 1NT : 2♣, 2◇ : 2♡ / 2♠ | Pass. |
| 1NT : any game bid | Pass. |
| 1NT : 2NT **or**<br>1NT : 2♣, 2◇ : 2NT. | a) Pass with minimum.<br>b) Bid 3NT with anything better. |
| 1NT : 3♡ / 3♠ **or**<br>1NT : 2♣, 2◇ : 3♡ / 3♠ | a) Raise to 4♡ / 4♠ with 3-card or better support.<br>b) Bid 3NT with 2-card support. |
| 1NT : 2♣, 2♡ : 3♡ **or**<br>1NT : 2♣, 2♠ : 3♠ | a) Pass with minimum hand.<br>b) Raise to 4-major if better. |
| 1NT : 2♣, 2♠ : 2NT | a) Pass with minimum.<br>b) Bid 3NT with anything better. |
| 1NT : 2♣, 2♠ : 3NT | Pass. |

## Rebids by the 1NT opener *continued*

| ON THE SEQUENCE: | OPENER SHOULD: |
|---|---|
| 1NT : 2♣, 2♡ : 2NT | With a minimum opening:<br>a) Bid 3♠ with four spades.<br>b) Pass without four spades.<br>With anything better:<br>c) Bid 4♠ with four spades.<br>d) Bid 3NT otherwise. |
| 1NT : 2♣, 2♡ : 3NT | a) Bid 4♠ with four spades.<br>b) Pass without four spades. |
| 1NT : 3♣ / 3◊ **or**<br>1NT : 2♣, 2-any : 3♣ or 3◊ | a) Raise with 4-card support.<br>b) Bid suit at 3-level.<br>c) Bid 3NT otherwise. |

Artificial rebids by responder for use in tournament play:

| 1NT : 2♣, 2♡ : 3♠ | Game-forcing heart raise with slam interest. Opener bids cheapest ace (cue-bid). |
|---|---|
| 1NT : 2♣, 2♠ : 3♡ | Game-forcing spade raise with slam interest. Opener bids cheapest ace (cue-bid). |

## Transfer bids

The schedule of responses to 1NT in the preceding pages is adequate for everyday use but a more sophisticated approach is favoured by many tournament players. It involves the use of transfer bids. Here is a simple system of transfer responses:

1NT : 2♣    Normal Stayman.
1NT : 2◊    Shows 5 or more hearts and asks opener to bid 2♡.
1NT : 2♡    Shows 5 or more spades and asks opener to bid 2♠.
1NT : 2♠    Shows a weak hand with a 6+ minor or a strong
            hand with both minors.
1NT : 2NT   Normal game-try.

When responder is weak, the use of transfers allows the lead to come up to the strong hand and keeps the strong hand concealed.

## Transfer bids *continued*

♠: 8 4   ♡: K 10 7 6 4 3   ◇: 8 5   ♣: Q J 5

In response to 1NT you bid 2◇, showing your heart suit. Opener rebids 2♡ and you pass, allowing partner to play the hand with the opening lead coming up to a possible tenace.

♠: Q J 9 8 4   ♡: 7   ◇: 10 3   ♣: Q 9 6 5 2

When partner opens 1NT you respond 2♡ and pass the 2♠ rebid, leaving partner to play the hand.

♠: 7 3   ♡: 8 4 2   ◇: 9   ♣: Q J 9 7 6 4 3

After an opening bid of 1NT you cannot play in a minor suit at the two-level* but you can do so at the three-level. With the above hand respond 2♠ and pass the forced rebid of 3♣. If your long suit were diamonds instead of clubs you would, of course, convert 3♣ to 3◇, which opener must pass.

A more important advantage of transfers becomes clear when responder has a stronger hand. The transfer sequence has the effect of creating an extra round of bidding, enabling responder to show cheaply several features, which are not available when the 2-level response is a sign-off.

♠: K J 6 4 2   ♡: A 7   ◇: 10 7 3   ♣: K 7 4

After a weak 1NT, respond 2♡ and continue with 2NT over the rebid of 2♠. You have shown five spades and the strength to invite game. Opener can now decide, based on the values and spade support held, whether to pass, sign off in 3♠, raise to 3NT or jump to 4♠. In all cases opener will be the declarer.

With a 6-card major and enough to invite game, transfer to the major and then raise to the 3-level:

♠: 8 6   ♡: Q 10 9 6 5 2   ◇: A J 3   ♣: K 7

Opposite a weak 1NT, bid 2◇ and after opener's 2♡, raise to 3♡ to invite game in hearts. With only a 5-card suit, you would have rebid 2NT and so the raise shows 6+ hearts.

---

*To play transfers but still be able to stop in 2◇, see *Bid Better, Much Better After Opening 1NT*, published by Weidenfeld & Nicolson / Peter Crawley.

# Transfer bids *continued*

With enough for game but no slam interest, you can transfer and bid game or change suit (forcing to game) after the transfer.

♠: K Q 9 8 7 4    ♡: 6    ◇: A 7 2    ♣: Q J 6

After 1NT, bid 2♡ and rebid 4♠ after opener's 2♠ rebid.

♠: A 5    ♡: A J 9 4 3    ◇: K Q    ♣: J 7 4 2

Respond 2◇ and jump to 3NT over the rebid of 2♡. You are offering a choice between 3NT and 4♡. With 3-card support opener will normally prefer the major-suit game.

♠: A K 8 7 4    ♡: Q 10 7 6 3    ◇: K 4    ♣: 2

On this hand start with 2♡ and jump to 4♡ over the 2♠ rebid. You are showing 5-5 in the majors with game values and opener can choose the suit.

## Breaking the transfer

After a transfer of 2◇ / 2♡ opener is expected to bid 2♡ / 2♠. With a superb fit for responder, opener is permitted to make some other bid. A superb fit has all three of these features:

● Support for responder's suit, and

● A doubleton elsewhere, and

● A maximum 1NT.

Opener's options to break the transfer are a jump to 3♡ / 3♠ *OR* bid a new suit which is very strong (two of the top three honours) *OR* bid 2NT to show two top honours in responder's suit and a 4-3-3-3 pattern, suggesting a no-trump contract.

## Responder changes suit

A transfer followed by a new suit is forcing to game. The second bid suit is natural. Opener can support the first suit (strongly at the 3-level, weakly at game-level), support the second suit (weakly by raising, strongly with a cue-bid) or bid 3NT with no support for either suit. Strong support implies two of the above three features which constitute a superb fit.

# Transfer bids *continued*

## After 1NT : 2♠, 3♣

Pass if weak with long clubs, bid 3◇ if weak with long diamonds. If responder is strong with both minors, the rebid is 3♡ (short in hearts), 3♠ (short in spades) or 3NT (2-2-4-5 or 2-2-5-4 with no slam interest). This helps opener to judge which game is best.

♠: A 4 3   ♡: 2   ◇: K Q 7 5   ♣: K J 4 3 2

After 1NT, bid 2♠ and over opener's 3♣, bid 3♡. This shows your suits and warns opener about the problem in hearts.

### Immediate jumps

Using transfers and Stayman you can show most strong hands. The problem type is the strong single-suiter with slam potential. With a 5-card minor, you can use Stayman and bid your suit at the 3-level; with a 5-card major, transfer and rebid 4NT or 5NT, but these paths are not ideal for a 6-card or longer suit.

1NT : 3♣ / 3◇ / 3♡ / 3♠ = 6+ suit, no second suit, forcing to game with slam potential. With poor support (10-x or worse), opener rebids 3NT. With decent support (J-x or better), opener bids the cheapest ace or raises the suit if no ace is held.

# Responding to 2NT (20-22 points, balanced shape)

If also balanced, responder adds up points in the normal way and passes with 0-3, bids 3NT with 4-10 and makes a slam try or a direct slam bid if stronger.

*Standard style responses:* A response of 3◇ / 3♡ / 3♠ shows a 5+ suit and is forcing to game. A game response is to be passed. A 3♣ response asks opener to bid the cheapest 4-card suit. Both partners then bid 4-card suits until a fit is found. If clubs is opener's only suit, the reply to 3♣ is 3NT.

*Transfer style responses:* 3◇ is a transfer to hearts, 3♡ is a transfer to spades, 3♠ shows both minors and slam interest. 4♣ / 4◇ = 6+ suit, forcing to game. A 3♣ response is Stayman, asking for a 4-card major.

24

## Responding to suit bids

**No-Trump responses** to an opening bid of one in a suit are normally made on balanced hands with two or three cards in partner's suit and no major suit that can be bid at the 1-level. *Exception:* The 1NT response to 1♢, 1♡ or 1♠ may be made on an unbalanced hand when no better response is available.

| POINTS | RESPONSE | NOTES |
|---|---|---|
| **0-5** | Pass | Little to gain by bidding. |
| **6-9** | 1NT | The 1NT response to 1♣ is expected to be a 3-3-3-4 pattern (4 clubs). |
| **10** | Bid a new suit | An awkward hand, too good for 1NT and not strong enough for 2NT. |
| **11-12** | 2NT | Inviting game, not forcing. For a different use of 2NT, see page 28. |
| **13-15** | 3NT | Should be a 4-3-3-3 pattern with no 4-card major and the unbid suits well stopped. |
| **16-up** | Bid a new suit | Either change suit, or jump-shift if that is warranted, and await developments. |

**Raises** normally promise 4-card support for opener's suit. Do not raise partner's minor if you have a major suit to show.

| POINTS | RESPONSE | NOTES |
|---|---|---|
| **0-5** | Generally pass | With 4 trumps and a singleton, raise with 3-5 points. |
| **6-9** | a) Single raise | You may raise 1♡ or 1♠ with 3 trumps and a ruffing value. |
| | b) Game raise | With 5 trumps and a void or singleton. |
| **10-12** | Jump raise | Inviting game with an 8-loser hand. |
| **13-up** | a) New suit | Bid game on the next round with 13-15 points (delayed game raise). |
| | b) 2NT | Jacoby Convention (see page 28). |
| | c) Jump-shift | (16+ points) and support next round. |

## Responding to suit bids *continued*

**Change of suit.** A response in a new suit is forcing for one round if responder is an unpassed hand. A change of suit by a passed hand is not forcing.

| POINTS | RESPONSE | NOTES |
|---|---|---|
| **0-5** | Generally pass | With 4 points and a 6+ suit, or 5 points and a 5-card suit, bid 1♡ / 1♠. |
| **6-15** | Bid one in a new suit | 6 points is the normal requirement for a for 1-level response. |
| **10-15** | Bid one or two in a new suit | 10 points is the normal requirement for a 2-level response in a lower-ranking suit but a 2-level response is permissible with 8-9 points and a good, long suit. |
| **16-up** | a) Bid one or two in a new suit | On two- or three-suited hands, which need plenty of bidding space for proper description and development. |
| | b) Jump in a new suit | If the hand fits the requirements for a jump-shift (see below). |

### Responder's jump-shift

Do not jump-shift just because you have 16 points or more. Expert practice nowadays is to restrict the jump-shift to three hand types:

1) A long, strong suit, such as K-Q-J-10-x-x or better, which has at most one loser expected, even opposite a singleton or void, *or*

2) A strong 5-card or longer suit as well as primary support for opener's suit, *or*

3) A strong 5-card suit in a balanced hand with stoppers in the unbid suits.

The requirement of 16 or more points can be shaded if the long, strong suit is solid and contains at least seven cards.

♠: A K Q J 9 8 4    ♡: A 4    ◇: 7 3    ♣: 9 2

After a 1♣ / 1◇ / 1♡ opening, bid 2♠ and follow with 4♠ to show a powerful suit but a minimum jump-shift.

# Responding to suit bids *continued*

**Pre-emptive responses** are made on weak hands that contain a playable 7-card or longer major suit.

| POINTS | RESPONSE | NOTES |
|--------|----------|-------|
| **3-7** | Double jump | e.g., 1♡ : 3♠ or 1♣ : 4♡ |

### Splinter responses

Pre-emptive responses below game have little popularity among top players (with a 7+ suit, bid your suit at the cheapest level and rebid it later). Splinter responses are preferred among tournament players. A splinter bid shows the values for game, 4+ support for partner and a singleton or void in the suit bid. A splinter bid is a double jump after partner's 1-level bid, such as 1♡ : 3♠, or a single jump after a 2-level response, such as 1♠ : 2♡, 4♣ or 1♠ : 2♣, 3♢. Opener's change of suit after a two-level response is forcing. As opener's jump-shift here is not needed in a natural sense, it can be used as a splinter.

♠:K Q 9 8 7   ♡:K 5 2   ♢:A 9 7 2   ♣:4

After a 1♠ opening, respond with a 4♣ splinter.

♠:K Q 9 8 7   ♡:A J 9 4   ♢:8   ♣:A J 2

After 1♠ : 2♡, continue with 4♢, a splinter raise of hearts.

♠:6   ♡:A K 9 4   ♢:K Q J 4 3   ♣:A 7 2

After 1♢ : 1♡, rebid 3♠, a splinter raise of hearts.

A splinter bid is forcing to game and should be considered as a short-suit try for slam. The K, Q and J are 'duplication' (wasted cards) opposite a singleton. Good holdings in the splinter suit are A-x-x, x-x-x or x-x-x-x. After discounting duplicated values, stay in game with a bare minimum for your bidding but look for slam with extra values.

♠:A Q 7 4 3   ♡:K 4   ♢:K Q 3   ♣:9 7 2

After 1♠ : 4♢, sign off in 4♠ (responder may bid further) but after 1♠ : 4♣ head for slam.

## Responding to suit bids *continued*

### The Jacoby 2NT convention

♠: K Q 7 5 3   ♡: A K   ◊: Q 7 5   ♣: 8 6 5

What should you respond with these cards if partner opens 1♠? To bid a fake 2♣ or 2◊ does not give partner a sensible impression of where your values lie. Strong hands with excellent support are hard to describe in natural methods. As a result many pairs have adopted the Jacoby 2NT response, which shows 13+ points, forcing to game, with 4+ support for opener.

With 4+ support, enough for game and a singleton or a void, give a splinter response. With the same values and support but no short suit, use the Jacoby 2NT response. There is no serious loss if you play Jacoby, since with 11-12 points balanced you can change suit and rebid 2NT on the next round. If you lack support for opener, there must be some 4-card suit to bid.

### Opener's rebids after the Jacoby 2NT response

● A new suit shows a singleton or a void. This should help responder judge whether there is slam potential.
● A jump to four in a new suit shows a good second suit, at least K-Q-x-x-x. This takes priority over showing a short suit.
● A jump to four of the agreed major is a minimum opening with no short suit. As a 4-3-3-3 or 4-4-3-2 hand will not be a minimum (would have opened 1NT with 12-14), the jump to 4-major promises at least a 5-card suit.
● A rebid of three of the agreed major promises a 5+ suit, no shortage and better than a minimum opening (so 14+ points).
● The 3NT rebid shows 15-17 points and only a 4-card suit.
● The 4NT rebid shows 18-19 points and only a 4-card suit.

**The Jacoby 2NT response** after a minor-suit opening. This is also forcing to game and denies a 4+ major suit. The rebids are the same (new suit is a short suit, jump in a new suit shows a strong second suit) except for the rebid of opener's minor at the 3-level. This shows a 5+ suit but need not be very strong since it may be vital to play in 3NT rather than 5-minor.

## Responder's choice of suit

Choose your response according to the following rules:
1) **With suits of unequal length** bid the longer first.

♠: Q 8 7 6 4   ♡: A K J 5   ◇: 8 3   ♣: 10 3

After a 1♣ or 1◇ opening, respond 1♠.

♠: K J 4 3   ♡: 6   ◇: A Q J 4 2   ♣: Q 6 2

After a 1♡ opening, respond 2◇. (After 1♣, respond 1◇.)

**Exception:** lacking the strength to respond at the 2-level in a lower-ranking suit, bid the shorter suit at the 1-level.

♠: A 9 8 3   ♡: 4 3   ◇: Q J 7 6 5   ♣: 5 2

After 1♡, respond 1♠. You are not strong enough for a 2◇ response. (After 1♣, respond 1◇.)

♠: 5   ♡: K 8 6 5 3   ◇: 9   ♣: K 10 9 7 4 3

After 1◇, respond 1♡. You are too weak for a 2♣ response.

2) **With 6-6 or 5-5 length** bid the higher-ranking suit first.

♠: A 8 5 4 3   ♡: A K J 5 2   ◇: 6   ♣: 8 2

After 1♣ or 1◇, respond 1♠.

♠: J 3   ♡: K J 8 7 2   ◇: A Q J 10 5   ♣: 2

After 1♣, bid 1♡. After 1♠, bid 2♡. 2♡ in response to 1♠ promises a 5-card or longer suit. A 2♣ or 2◇ response does not.

3) **With no suit longer than four cards** bid the cheapest suit.

♠: A K 10 5   ♡: J 10 6 2   ◇: 9 7 3   ♣: 8 7

After 1♣ or 1◇, bid 1♡.

♠: 6   ♡: A Q 5 2   ◇: K Q 7 3   ♣: Q J 7 2

After 1♠, respond 2♣.

4) **With a major suit and support for a minor** bid the major.
♠: 10 5   ♡: K J 6 2   ◇: 9 7   ♣: K 9 7 4 3

After 1♣, bid 1♡. (After 1◇, bid 1♡. After 1♠, bid 1NT.)

# Rebids by the opener

The opening bid of one in a suit has a wide range, from 10 to 20 points. The rebid defines strength and shape more closely.

## 1) After a response of 1NT (6-9 points)

| POINTS | OPENER SHOULD |
|---|---|
| **14 *or less*** | a) Pass with a balanced or semi-balanced hand.<br>b) Rebid a 6-card suit at the 2-level.<br>c) Bid a lower-ranking suit at the 2-level. |
| **15-16** | a) Pass with a balanced or semi-balanced hand.<br>b) Jump to three in a good 6-card suit (invitational).<br>c) Raise to 2NT with a good 6-card minor.<br>d) Bid a new suit at the 2-level. |
| **17-18** | a) Bid 2NT with a balanced or semi-balanced hand.<br>b) Jump to three in a 6-card or longer major with six losers (invitational).<br>c) Jump to four in a strong 6-card or longer major with five losers.<br>d) Bid 3♣ / 3◇ or 3NT with a good 6-card minor.<br>e) Bid a new suit at the 2-level.<br>f) Jump to three in a lower-ranking 5+ suit.<br>g) After opening 1♠, jump to 4♡ with a 6-5 pattern. (If 5-5, jump to 3♡ and remove 3NT to 4♡.) |
| **19-up** | a) Bid 3NT with a balanced or semi-balanced hand.<br>b) Jump to 4-of-your-major with a good 6+ suit.<br>c) Bid a new, higher-ranking suit at the 2-level.<br>d) Jump to three in a new, lower-ranking suit. |

## The reverse bid

A 2-level rebid in a higher-ranking suit is called a reverse. It is forcing for one round and should not be made with fewer than 15 points, as responder may have to give preference at the 3-level.

♠: A K 9 4    ♡: K Q 8 7 2    ◇: K J 5    ♣: 6

After 1♡ : 1NT, rebid 2♠. Without the ◇K, rebid 2♡ or pass.

# Rebids by the opener *continued*

## 2) **After a natural response of 2NT** (11-12 points)

POINTS      OPENER SHOULD

**13** *or*    a) Pass except with a very distributional hand.
*less*        b) Rebid three in a 6-card suit with 10-12 points.
              This is a sign-off.
              c) Bid four in a 7-card major, or in a 6-card major
              with 12-13 points and good controls.
              d) Bid three in a new 5-card suit. This is forcing for
              one round.

**14-up**     a) Bid 3NT with a balanced hand, or a semi-balanced
              hand with no slam ambitions.
              b) Bid four in a 6-card major with no slam prospects.
              c) Bid three in a new suit. If near-maximum, make a
              slam try on the next round if a trump fit is found.

♠: K 8 4   ♡: Q 10 9 6 5 3   ◇: K Q   ♣: 8 2

After 1♡ : 2NT, sign off in 3♡. Add a king and you bid 4♡.

## 3) **After a natural response of 3NT** (13-15, 4-3-3-3 pattern)

POINTS      OPENER SHOULD

**15** *or*    a) Bid four in a 6-card major, or in a 5-card major if
*less*        holding a void, singleton or two doubletons.
              b) Bid a new 5-card suit at the 4-level.
              c) Otherwise pass.

**16-up**     a) Pass with a balanced 16-17.
              b) Raise to 4NT with a balanced 18-19.
              c) Rebid a 6-card minor at the 4-level (slam try).
              d) Bid a new minor suit at the 4-level (slam try).
              e) Jump to five in a 6-card major (slam try).
              f) Bid slam direct.

♠: A K Q 7 4   ♡: 8 3   ◇: A Q 8 6 3   ♣: A

After 1♠ : 3NT, bid 4◇. There could be a grand slam.

# Rebids by the opener *continued*

### 4) **After a single raise** (6-9 points)

The point count alone is not adequate. Opener should revalue the hand in terms of the Losing Trick Count (see page 9). After a single raise in a major suit, the general rule for the opener is to pass with 7 losers (or worse), try for game with 5½-6 losers and to jump to game with 5 losers or fewer.

♠: A K 8 6 4   ♡: 2   ◇: A Q J 7 5   ♣: 9 7

After 1♠ : 2♠, opener with 5 losers should bid 4♠.

♠: A K 8 6 4   ♡: 8 6 4   ◇: A Q J   ♣: 9 7

After 1♠ : 2♠, opener with 7 losers should pass.

**Trial bids:** With 5½-6 losers, opener suggests game in a major by bidding a new suit, which may be only of 3-card length. This is forcing for one round.

♠: 4   ♡: A J 8 7 6 3   ◇: Q 7 5   ♣: A K 4

After 1♡ : 2♡, opener makes a trial bid of 3◇, the suit where help is needed. The focus is now on responder's holding in diamonds. Responder is expected to bid game in the major if able to help in the trial suit, otherwise to sign off by bidding three of the agreed major. A good guide for the trial suit holding:

| RESPONDER HOLDS | RESPONDER SHOULD BID |
| --- | --- |
| **0-1 loser** | Game in the major. A void or ace -singleton is no loser. Other singletons or K-x / A-x or K-Q-x / A-Q-x / A-K-x = 1 loser. |
| **2 losers** | 4-major if maximum, 3-major if minimum. Q-x doubleton or worse = 2 losers and so are Q-x-x, K-x-x or A-x-x (or longer). |
| **3 losers** | 3-major as a sign-off. J-x-x or worse holdings in a 3+ suit = 3 losers. |

After 1♣ : 2♣ or 1◇ : 2◇, a new suit is played as a stopper bid in the quest for 3NT as a possible game, not as a trial bid.

# Rebids by the opener *continued*

## Opener's rebid after a single raise

POINTS    OPENER SHOULD

**16** *or*
*less*
a) Pass with a balanced hand.
b) Make a trial bid with a major suit as trumps and holding 5½-6 losers.
c) Bid game in agreed major if holding 4-5 losers.

**17-18**
a) Bid 2NT with a balanced hand.
b) With an agreed major, make a trial bid with 6 losers.
c) Bid game in agreed major if holding 4-5½ losers.
d) With an agreed minor, make a stopper bid.

**19-20**
a) Bid 3NT with a balanced hand.
b) Make a stopper bid with an agreed minor suit.
c) Bid game in a 5-card or longer major.

## 5) After 1♡ : 3♡ or 1♠ : 3♠

POINTS    OPENER SHOULD

**13** *or*
*less*
a) Pass with poor controls, such as:
♠: J 5    ♡: K Q 9 6 5 3    ◇: A 9 3    ♣: J 4
♠: K J 10 6 2    ♡: Q J 4    ◇: K Q 5    ♣: 8 7
b) Bid game in major with good controls, such as:
♠: A J 8 6 5    ♡: K 7 2    ◇: A 7 4 3    ♣: 6

**14-up**
a) Bid 3NT if 4-3-3-3, else bid game in the major.
b) Head for slam if maximum with good controls.

## 6) After 1♣ : 3♣ or 1◇ : 3◇

POINTS    OPENER SHOULD

**14** *or*
*less*
a) Generally pass.
b) With excellent shape and 4-5 losers bid 5♣ / 5◇.

**15-up**
a) Bid 3NT if balanced.
b) Make a stopper bid at the 3-level.
c) Head for slam if maximum with good controls.

7) **After 1♡ : 4♡ or 1♠ : 4♠** opener should pass unless strong with excellent controls and exceptionally shapely.

# Rebids by the opener *continued*

## 8) **After a response of one in a suit**

| POINTS | OPENER SHOULD |
|---|---|

**14** *or*
*less*
a) Raise responder's suit to the 2-level.
b) Bid one in a new suit.
c) Bid two in a lower-ranking suit.
d) Rebid a 6-card suit or a very strong 5-card suit.

**15-16**
a) Raise responder's suit to the 3-level with 4-card support and a singleton or two doubletons.
b) Raise responder's major to the 2-level with less support or less shape.
c) Bid one in a new suit.
d) Bid two in a new suit.
e) Bid 1NT with a balanced hand.
f) Rebid a 6-card suit, at the 2-level with 6½-7 losers, at the 3-level with 5½-6 losers, at the 4-level with a self-sufficient suit and 4-5 losers.

**17-18**
a) Raise responder's major to the 3-level with 4-card support and 5½-6 losers, to the 4-level with 4-5 losers.
b) Rebid in no-trumps if balanced (1NT or 2NT, depending on your methods – see pages 14-15).
c) Bid one in a new suit.
d) Raise responder's minor to the 3-level.
e) Bid two in a new suit.
f) Rebid a 6-card suit, at the 3-level with 5½-6 losers, at the 4-level with a self-sufficient suit and 4-5 losers.

**19-up**
a) Jump to game in responder's major with 4-card support (or make a splinter bid – see page 27).
b) Jump-rebid to 2NT (forcing) with a balanced hand (see page 15).
c) Make a reverse bid, forcing for one round.
d) Jump in a new suit (jump-shift), forcing to game.
e) Jump to game in your suit with a self-sufficient suit. Add the number of cards in the suit to the honour cards in the suit. If the total is 10+, the suit is self-sufficient.

# Rebids by the opener *continued*

## 9) After a response of two in a lower-ranking suit

POINTS   OPENER SHOULD

**14** *or*   a) Raise 1♠ : 2♡ to 3♡ with 3+ support.
*less*   b) Raise a minor suit response to three with 4-card
   support or with 14 points and 3-card support.
   c) Bid two in a lower-ranking new suit (forcing).
   d) Repeat a 5+ suit as the least attractive choice.

**15-16**   a) With 3-card support, raise 1♠ : 2♡ to 4♡. With
   4+ support, raise to 4♡ or give a splinter raise.
   b) Bid 2NT with a balanced hand.
   c) Bid any new suit (forcing).
   d) Raise a minor suit to the 3-level with support.
   e) Jump to three in a good 6+ suit.
   f) Jump to game in your suit with a self-sufficient suit.

**17-up**   a) With 3-card support, raise 1♠ : 2♡ to 4♡. With
   4+ support, raise to 4♡ or give a splinter raise.
   b) Bid 3NT with 18-19 and a 4-3-3-3 pattern.
   c) Bid 2NT with any other balanced hand.
   d) Bid any new suit (forcing).
   e) Raise a minor suit response to the 4-level with
   4-card support (forcing) or give a splinter raise.
   f) Jump to game in a self-sufficient major suit.

## 10) After a jump-shift

The jump-response in a new suit is unconditionally forcing to
game. If playing the jump-shift style outlined on page 26,
opener should usually make the cheapest bid and responder's
rebid will clarify the nature of the jump-shift. Exceptionally,
opener may rebid the suit opened with a self-sufficient suit.

If not playing jump-shifts in such a disciplined manner, opener
should rebid naturally (one level higher than normal). Jumps
by opener have a special meaning. A jump-rebid of opener's
suit shows a solid 6+ suit with little extra. A jump-raise of
responder's suit shows 4-card support and a minimum opening.

## Rebids by the responder

### 1) **After opener's minimum rebid in the suit opened**

| POINTS | RESPONDER SHOULD |
|---|---|
| **8** *or less* | Generally pass. |

**9-10**
a) Rebid a good 6-card suit.
b) Bid a second 5-card suit at the 2-level.
c) Raise opener's major to the 3-level with three trumps and a singleton or two doubletons.
d) Otherwise pass.

**11-12**
a) Bid 2NT with the unbid suits stopped.
b) Bid a new suit at the 2-level.
c) Raise opener's suit to the 3-level with three trumps or with a doubleton honour.
d) Jump in a good 6-card major.

**13-15**
a) Bid 3NT with the unbid suits stopped.
b) Raise opener's major to the 4-level with three trumps or with a doubleton honour.
c) Jump to game in a self-sufficient major suit.
d) Bid any new suit.

**16-up**
a) With no slam potential, bid any obvious game.
b) If the right spot is not obvious, change suit.

### 2) **After opener's jump-rebid in the suit opened**

This is droppable after a 1-level response but any bid by responder is game-forcing. With 8+ points bid again: 3NT with the unbid suits stopped, raise opener's major with 2 trumps or Q-singleton or better, rebid a 6-card suit at the 3-level or bid any new suit.

### 3) **When opener rebids 1NT, showing 15-16 balanced**

| POINTS | RESPONDER SHOULD |
|---|---|
| **8** *or less* | a) Pass with a balanced hand. |

b) Rebid a 6-card suit.
c) Bid a new 5-card suit at the two-level.
d) Bid two in opener's suit with support.
e) Jump to 4-major with 8 points and a good 6+ suit.

# Rebids by the responder *continued*

## 3) When opener rebids 1NT, showing 15-16 points *continued*

| POINTS | RESPONDER SHOULD |
|---|---|
| **9** | a) Bid 2NT if balanced or with length in the minors. |
| | b) Jump to four in a 6-card major. |
| | c) Jump to three in any suit (forcing). |
| **10-15** | a) Bid 3NT if balanced or with length in the minors. |
| | b) Jump to four in a 6-card major. |
| | c) Jump to three in any suit (forcing). |
| **16-up** | a) Bid 4NT with 17 points balanced, inviting 6NT. |
| | b) Bid 6NT with a balanced 18-20. |
| | c) Bid 5NT with a balanced 21-22, inviting 7NT. |
| | d) Bid 7NT with a balanced 23 or more. |
| | e) Jump to three in any suit (forcing). |

When the 1NT rebid shows 15-17 or 15-18, most pairs use 2♣ by responder with 8+ points to ask opener for more information.* Opener rebids:

2♦ = artificial, absolutely minimum, 15 points only.

2♥ / 2♠ / 2NT = medium range, 16 points or 15 plus a 5-card suit. With options, opener bids the cheapest feature. For example, after 1♣ : 1♠, 1NT : 2♣, opener with 16 points would bid 2♥ with four hearts, 2♠ with three spades (denying four hearts) or 2NT (denying four hearts and denying three spades). Any 3-level bid = maximum, 17 points or 17-18 points.

After opener's 2-level rebid, responder must jump to the 3-level to force opener to bid again.

Other than 2♣, responder's 2-level new suit lower-ranking than the first suit is not encouraging, e.g., 1♣ : 1♠, 1NT : 2♥. Because the 2♣ check-back ascertains opener's point count, a natural 2NT rebid is not needed. Instead the 2NT rebid asks opener to bid 3♣. This enables responder to sign off in clubs.

---

*For an alternative and highly attractive approach after opener's 1NT rebid, whereby responder describes the values and suits held instead of asking for opener's strength and features, see Appendix 1 in *The Power of Shape*, also published by Weidenfeld & Nicolson / Peter Crawley.

## Rebids by the responder *continued*

### 4) **When opener rebids 2NT after a two-level response**

Responder can go straight to game, bid a new suit or support opener's suit.

### 5) **When opener makes a jump-rebid of 2NT**

If this is played as 17-18, responder may pass or sign off in the responded suit. Otherwise responder can bid game or make a forcing bid by bidding a new suit or supporting opener's suit.

The popular modern approach is to play the jump to 2NT as 18-19 or 19-20 and forcing. Further bidding is natural.

### 6) **When opener makes a jump-rebid of 3NT**

This is best played as 19-20 and a 4-3-3-3 pattern. With a weak hand responder should pass or rebid a 5+ major. Any other bid is a slam try.

### 7) **When opener raises a 1NT response to 2NT**

Pass with 6 or 7 points, bid 3NT with 8 or 9 or sign off in a new suit with 5-7 points and a 6+ suit.

### 8) **When opener raises a one-level response to two**

| POINTS | RESPONDER SHOULD |
|---|---|
| **6-7** | Pass except with freakish distribution. |
| **8-9** | a) Pass if balanced or if the agreed suit is a minor.<br>b) Bid 3 with 8 losers if the suit is a major. |
| **10-12** | a) If the suit is a major, raise to the 3-level or make a trial bid.<br>b) If the suit is a minor, bid 2NT with the other suits stopped or make a stopper bid in a new suit.<br>c) With 7 losers, bid game if the suit is a major. |
| **13-15** | a) Bid game in a 5-card or longer major.<br>b) Bid 3NT with the other suits stopped.<br>c) Bid a new suit. |

# Rebids by the responder *continued*

### 9) **When opener raises a 2-level response to three**

Pass if absolutely minimum, otherwise head for game. If the suit is a minor, you can bid a new suit as a stopper, give 3-card support for opener's major, bid 3NT / 5-minor or look for slam.

### 10) **When opener raises a 1-level response to three**

Responder may pass with 6-7 points and a 4-card suit. If the suit raised is a major, bid game with 8 or more points or look for slam with 13 or more. If the suit is a minor, try a new suit (stopper) or bid 3NT with a scattered 8 points.

### 11) **When opener raises a 2-level response to four**

Generally pass if the suit is hearts but consider a slam try with 12+ points and good controls. The double raise to four of a minor is forcing to game. You can show delayed support for opener's major or bid five of the minor or make a slam try.

### 12) **When opener raises a 1-level response to four**

Consider a slam try with 10 or more points and good controls.

### 13) **When opener bids a new suit after a 1-level response**

PREFERENCE

With a weak hand, responder is expected to show preference for one of opener's suit. That can be done by passing with greater length in opener's second suit or by returning to opener's first suit at minimum level with equal length in the two suits or greater length in opener's first suit. Suppose opener bids 1♡ and rebids 2♢ after your response of 1♠:

♠: K 10 7 6 3　♡: 8 2　♢: 8 7 2　♣: K 4 3　　Pass.
♠: K 10 7 6 3　♡: 8 2　♢: K 8　♣: 9 4 3 2　　Bid 2♡.

With 10-12 points, give jump-preference to the 3-level. Opener bids 1♢ and rebids 1♠ over your response of 1♡:

♠: J 9 4 3　♡: A Q 8 4　♢: K J　♣: 8 7 2　Bid 3♠.
♠: J 9　♡: A Q 8 4　♢: K J 3 2　♣: 8 7 2　Bid 3♢.

## Rebids by the responder *continued*

After opener rebids in a new suit at the 1-level:

POINTS   RESPONDER SHOULD

**6-9**      a) Raise the second suit to two with 4-card support.
             b) Bid two of opener's first suit with 3+ support.
             c) Rebid your own 6+ suit.
             d) Rebid 1NT.

**10-12**    a) With support and 8 losers, raise one of opener's suits
             to the 3-level.
             b) With 4-card support and 7 losers, raise opener's
             major suit to game.
             c) Bid 2NT with a stopper in the unbid suit.
             d) Jump to the 3-level with your own good 6-card suit.
             e) Bid game in your major with a self-sufficient suit.

**13-15**    a) With support, raise to game in opener's major.
             b) Bid game in your major with a self-sufficient suit.
             c) Bid 3NT with the unbid suit well-stopped.
             d) Otherwise, bid the fourth suit to force to game.

### 14) **Opener bids a new suit (forcing) after a 2-level response**

POINTS   RESPONDER SHOULD

**8-9**      a) Return to opener's major at the 2-level (not forcing).
             b) Repeat a 6+ minor (not forcing).

**10-12**    a) Bid 2NT with a stopper in the unbid suit.
             b) Raise the second suit to three with 4-card support.
             c) Give jump-preference to the 3-level with 3-card
             support for opener's major and 8 losers.
             d) Bid game in opener's major with support and 7 losers.
             e) Repeat a 6+ minor.
             None of the above actions is forcing.

**13-15**    a) With support, raise to game in a major.
             b) Bid 3NT with the unbid suit well-stopped.
             c) Otherwise bid the fourth suit to force to game.

# Rebids by the responder *continued*

## 15) **When opener shows reversing values**

A reverse is a new suit *at the 2-level* in a suit higher-ranking than the suit opened. Opener's rebid in these auctions is a reverse:
1♣ : 1♠, 2♦ ...   1♡ : 1NT, 2♠ ...   1♦ : 2♣, 2♡...

After a suit opening, 2-of-opener's-suit is a notional barrier. A new suit below the 'barrier' does not promise extra strength, but a new suit beyond opener's barrier does.

A new suit rebid at the 2-level will not be a reverse if the bidding is already beyond opener's barrier. For example:

| W | N | E | S | |
|---|---|---|---|---|
| 1♣ | 1♡ | 2♦ | No | 2♠ is not a reverse and does not promise extra values. East's 2♦ |
| 2♠ ... | | | | is already beyond the 2♣ barrier. |

After a 2-level response a reverse is forcing to game.
After a 1-level response a reverse is forcing for one round.
Responder's non-forcing rebids then are:
a) 2NT, 5-8 points with a stopper in the fourth suit.
b) A minimum rebid in responder's suit.
c) Simple preference to opener's first suit.
d) Raising 2♦, opener's second suit, to 3♦.
All other rebids by responder show 9+ points and force to game.

After a 2-level response opener's new-suit rebid at the 3-level promises 15+ points and is forcing to game.

## 16) **Opener jumps in a new suit**
Opener's jump-shift is forcing to game. Further bidding is natural.

### **Fast arrival and slow arrival**
In a game-forcing auction, supporting partner's suit below game is stronger than jumping to game, e.g., after 1♡ : 2♣, 2♠ responder's 3♡ / 3♠ rebids are stronger than 4♡ / 4♠.

### **1-minor : 1♡, 2♡ : 2NT or 1-suit : 1♠, 2♠ : 2NT**
Responder's 2NT after a major suit raise asks whether opener has four trumps. Opener rebids the major with four (3-level minimum, 4-level maximum) or bids another suit with three.

# Acol two-bids

An opening bid of 2◇, 2♡ or 2♠ denotes a powerful hand better than eight playing tricks (4-4½ losers). These are hands on which game may be missed if the opening bid is one in a suit. With a bare eight playing tricks you can afford to open with a one-bid. You need partner to have more than one trick to make game and with that much, partner will respond to a one-opening.

For an Acol two the hand may be single-suited or two-suited. The point count is usually around the 17-20 mark but can range from 14-22. These are examples of an Acol two:

| | | | | |
|---|---|---|---|---|
| ♠: A K Q 9 8 7 3 | ♡: 3 | ◇: A J 10 | ♣: 9 2 | Open 2♠ |
| ♠: A J 10 8 2 | ♡: A K | ◇: K Q J 5 4 | ♣: 5 | Open 2♠ |
| ♠: A Q J 9 7 | ♡: A K Q 5 3 2 | ◇: 9 | ♣: 3 | Open 2♡ |
| ♠: 4 | ♡: A Q 7 | ◇: K Q J 10 6 5 | ♣: A K 6 | Open 2◇ |

## Negative response

The Acol two-bid is forcing for one round. The negative response, 0-7 points, is 2NT, which denies the ability to make any constructive move. Having given a negative response, the responder may pass a simple rebid or minimum change of suit on the next round. Opener must jump below game or reverse at the 3-level to force responder to bid again. (Some play that change of suit by opener is forcing. Check this with partner.) Of course, responder may well bid again despite a negative response, especially if at the top end of the negative range.

Suppose the bidding starts 2♠ : 2NT, 3◇ and you hold:

| | | | | |
|---|---|---|---|---|
| ♠: 7 | ♡: J 8 7 2 | ◇: 8 5 4 | ♣: J 10 4 3 2 | Pass |
| ♠: 8 2 | ♡: 9 7 4 3 | ◇: 6 3 | ♣: Q 8 5 3 2 | Bid 3♠ |
| ♠: 8 3 2 | ♡: K 5 3 2 | ◇: 9 | ♣: 7 6 5 4 2 | Bid 4♠ |
| ♠: 8 2 | ♡: 9 7 4 | ◇: K J 6 3 | ♣: 6 5 4 2 | Bid 4◇ |
| ♠: 8 | ♡: K 5 | ◇: Q 9 7 5 3 | ♣: 8 7 5 4 2 | Bid 5◇ |

# Acol two-bids *continued*

**Positive response**

Any positive response is forcing to game.

a) Single raise

Denotes trump support and an ace. The hand may be either weak (relatively) or strong.

Opener bids 2♠ and you hold:

♠: Q 8 2   ♡: 5   ◇: A 9 6 5   ♣: 10 8 7 4 2    Raise to 3♠

You do not plan to move for slam unless partner indicates some slam interest next.

♠: K 5 3   ♡: A K 8 4   ◇: K 7 5 4   ♣: Q 5    Raise to 3♠

You plan to look for slam even if partner bids 4♠ next, but for the moment you simply set the trump suit.

b) Double raise

Shows trump support with two second-round controls (kings or singletons) but no ace.

Opener bids 2♡ and you hold:

♠: 8 7 5   ♡: K 9 7   ◇: K Q 7 4   ♣: 10 4 3    Raise to 4♡

Any further move is up to partner.

♠: 7   ♡: Q 9 6 2   ◇: 7 6 5 4 2   ♣: K J 3    Raise to 4♡

(A useful approach for this hand if playing splinters would be to jump to 3♠ to show a positive response with 4+ support and a singleton or void in the suit bid. Note that splinters are not compatible with the solid-suit jump under e) below.)

c) Bid a new suit: Shows a good 5-card or longer suit and 8 points or more. 7 points will do if that includes 1½ quick tricks.

d) Jump to 3NT: Indicates a balanced hand with 10-12 points. If weaker, bid 2NT first and rebid 3NT with sufficient strength if no trump fit has been located. If stronger, start with a suit bid and head for slam later.

e) Jump in a new suit: Shows a solid suit (A-K-Q-J-3-2).

## Opening 2♣

The artificial opening bid of 2♣ is reserved for the most powerful hands of all, balanced hands with at least 23 points, and unbalanced hands with at least 20 points and better than nine playing tricks (3½ losers or fewer). Each of these hands qualifies for an opening bid of 2♣.

♠: A Q J 8 4  ♡: A K Q 5  ◇: A Q J  ♣: 9

♠: K Q 7  ♡: A Q 9 6  ◇: - - -  ♣: A K Q J 6 3

♠: A 9  ♡: K J 10 6 4 3  ◇: A  ♣: A K J 6

♠: A J 7  ♡: A Q  ◇: A K Q 7 2  ♣: K 3 2

♠: A K  ♡: K J 4  ◇: A Q 8 3  ♣: A K Q 9

### Negative response

The negative response with a weak hand (less than 8 points) is an artificial 2◇. The opener rebids naturally, showing a 5+ suit or bidding no-trumps, according to strength. On the above hands the rebids after a negative 2◇ response would be 2♠, 3♣, 2♡, 2NT and 3NT respectively.

### Exceptional case

The 2♣ opening is forcing to game with one exception. After a negative response and a rebid of 2NT, showing 23-24 points, responder may pass with a hopeless hand (0-2 points). Even then responder may try for a 4♡ or 4♠ with a 6-card major. With as much as 3 points or one queen, responder should bid again, responding in the same manner as to a 2NT opening bid.

| | W | E | |
|---|---|---|---|
| ♠A K Q 7 4 | 2♣ | 2◇ | ♠8 5 |
| ♡A K J 5 3 | | | ♡7 6 4 2 |
| ◇A 5 | 2♠ | 2NT | ◇9 8 3 |
| ♣Q | 3♡ | 4♡ | ♣8 7 6 3 |
| | No | | |

It would be a serious error for East to pass 2♠. An easy game in 4♡ would be missed. After a 2◇ negative if unable to support opener's suit, rebid in your own 5+ suit or bid 2NT on a hand without 3+ support for opener and no 5+ suit of your own.

| ♠ A Q J 2 | W | E | ♠ 8 5 |
|---|---|---|---|
| ♡ A 5 | 2♣ | 2♢ | ♡ 9 8 7 6 4 3 2 |
| ♢ A K 7 | 2NT | 4♡ | ♢ 9 8 |
| ♣ K Q 3 2 | No | | ♣ 8 7 |

Playing transfers after 2NT, the bidding would go:
2♣ : 2♢, 2NT : 3♢ (transfer), 3♡ : 4♡.

| ♠ A K Q J 7 6 | W | E | ♠ 5 |
|---|---|---|---|
| ♡ A K Q J 7 4 | 2♣ | 2♢ | ♡ 9 8 3 2 |
| ♢ A | 2♠ | 2NT | ♢ 7 6 3 2 |
| ♣ - - - | 7♡ | No | ♣ 9 5 3 2 |

In a tournament one West unwisely opened 7♠ and paid the price when spades were 5-1. By showing both suits West enlists East's co-operation in selecting the better trump suit.

## Positive responses to 2♣

A positive response promises 8 points or more, or 7 points including 1½ quick tricks (see page 11 for quick tricks).

a) 2♡ / 2♠ / 3♣ / 3♢

Positive response with at least a 5-card suit. With more than one suit, bid the longer suit first or the higher-ranking suit when holding a 5-5 or 6-6 pattern.

b) 2NT   Balanced 7-9 points.

c) 3NT   Balanced 10-12 points.

d) 3♡ / 3♠ / 4♣ / 4♢      Solid suit (A-K-Q-J-3-2 or better).

A positive response indicates slam is likely, especially if a trump fit is found. If not playing splinters, later jumps by responder show long suits with one or two losers:

2♣ : 2♠, 3♡ : 4♠   After a positive response, this jump-rebid shows a 1-loser suit (A-Q-J-10-3-2 or K-Q-J-10-3-2).

2♣ : 2♢, 2♠ : 4♡   After a negative response, the jump-rebid shows a 2-loser suit (Q-J-10-9-3-2 or K-J-10-9-3-2).

## Weak Two-Bids

Many players, particularly in tournament play, have abandoned Acol two-bids in favour of weak two-bids in the major suits. Such bids have a mild pre-emptive effect and a good way to look at them is as pre-empts with a 6-card suit.

The requirements for a weak two-bid are 6-10 points and a good 6-card major suit. It is best to adhere to strict standards. The suit should be headed by Q-J or Q-10-9 or better, the hand should not contain a void or two singletons and the opener should not hold four cards in the other major.

### Responses

Raises of the major suit are pre-emptive and must be passed by opener. It is sensible to raise to the 3-level with three trumps and 8-13 points and to the 4-level with four trumps, regardless of strength if there is no slam potential. If your side has ten trumps, the other side must have a good trump fit as well, either a 9-card or better fit or two 8-card fits.

A new suit response is forcing, asking for a raise with 3-card support or with a Q-x or better doubleton. The response of 2NT is the Ogust Convention, a range-and-quality inquiry, to which the opener rebids as follows:

3♣ = minimum range (6-8) and a moderate suit.
3◇ = minimum range (6-8) and a good suit.
3♡ = maximum range (9-10) and a moderate suit.
3♠ = maximum range (9-10) and a good suit.
3NT = best possible suit, A-K-Q-x-x-x and little more.

To look for game with no support for opener, you need 16+ points. With support, you should have better than 3 tricks as the weak-two opener normally has 7-8 losers. Count the ace, king or queen in the opener's suit as one trick each, add your quick tricks and add two tricks for an outside void and one for a singleton. With 3½-4 tricks, use 2NT but bid 3-major if opener is minimum. With 4½-5½ tricks, bid game. With 6+ tricks, use 2NT and explore slam possibilities.

# Benjamin Two-Bids

There is no need to make a straight choice between Acol twos and weak twos. Using a convention designed by Albert Benjamin of Scotland it is possible to have the best of both worlds. The Benjamin structure of two-bids is as follows:

2♣  Shows an Acol two-bid (i.e., a powerful hand with 8½-9½ playing tricks (3½-4½ losers) in any of the four suits. One advantage is that opener can show an Acol-two type with clubs as the dominant suit. The negative response with 0-7 points is 2◇. Any other response is natural and forcing to game. After a negative response, responder will normally bid again with 4-7 points or with a sure trick or better.

Opener's suit rebids after 2♣ : 2◇
  New suit = 5+ suit (3♣ or 3◇ are usually 6+ suits).
  3♡ / 3♠ = good 6+ suit and only 4 losers.
  4♡ / 4♠ = strong 6+ suit and 3½ losers.

2◇  Shows the equivalent of an Acol 2♣ opening, with the small disadvantage that the bidding starts one step higher. The negative response is 2♡ and a game-forcing situation exists except where opener rebids 2NT (23-24 points balanced).

2♡ / 2♠  These are weak two-bids, showing 6-10 points and a good 6-card suit. See opposite page for details.

Another advantage of Benjamin twos is that it is easy to define strong hands within a narrow range. Here are two options:

| Structure 1: | Points | Structure 2: | Points |
|---|---|---|---|
| 2NT | = 19-20 | 2NT | = 21-22 |
| 2♣ : 2◇, 2NT | = 21-22 | 2♣ : 2◇, 2NT | = 23-24 |
| 2◇ : 2♡, 2NT | = 23-24 | 2◇ : 2♡, 2NT | = 25-28 |
| 2♣ : 2◇, 3NT | = 25-26 | 2◇ : 2♡, 3NT | = 29-30 |
| 2◇ : 2♡, 3NT | = 27-28 | | |

A benefit in structure 2 is that opener can rebid a game-forcing 2NT after opening 2◇. The 2♣ : 2◇, 3NT sequence can then be used to show a 9-trick hand with a solid minor, such as:

♠: A  ♡: A 3  ◇: 7 6 2  ♣: A K Q J 7 5 2

# The Multi-2♦ Opening

Many tournament players like to play an artificial 2♦ opening which has several meanings (hence the name 'multi'). In most cases the 2♦ includes a weak two in hearts or a weak two in spades as two of the options. These are popular schemes:
1) A weak two in one of the majors as the only option.
2) A weak two in either major *OR* an Acol-two in either minor *OR* a balanced 23-24.
3) A weak two in either major *OR* a 4-4-4-1 or 5-4-4-0 of 19+ points *OR* a balanced 23-24.

### Responding with a weak hand

Responder will usually bid 2♥, asking opener to pass with a weak two in hearts or otherwise describe the hand held. Over 2♥, opener can bid 2♠ (weak two in spades), 2NT (the 23-24 balanced hand) or bid at the 3-level to reveal other strong options. With a strong fit for hearts and a poor fit for spades, responder with a weak hand might bid 2♠, saying 'Please pass with a weak two in spades, otherwise show your holding. With a weak two in hearts, bid 3♥ if minimum, 4♥ if maximum.'

### Responding with a strong hand

A minor suit response is natural and forcing. The most common strong action is the 2NT inquiry. The standard replies are:
3♣ = maximum weak two in hearts.
3♦ = maximum weak two in spades.
3♥ = minimum weak two in hearts.
3♠ = minimum weak two in spades.
A strong option opposite a 2NT reply is enough for slam.

A very useful alternative set of replies, which allow responder to play the hand when opener is weak works like this:
3♣ =  weak two in hearts.
3♦ =  weak two in spades.
3♥ / 3♠ =  8½ - 9 playing tricks in the major bid.
After 3♣ responder can invite game with 3♥ or jump to 4♥.
After 3♦ responder can invite game with 3♠ or jump to 4♠.

# The 2♡ and 2♠ openings when playing 2◇-multi

If your multi-2◇ opening includes a weak two in hearts and a weak two in spades among the options, how should you use the 2♡ and 2♠ openings? One option is to play them as the Acol-two types (and include an Acol-two in a minor among the strong options for the 2◇ opening). Another possibility, attractive for duplicate players, is to play them as weak two-suiters, showing 6-10 points with 5+ cards in the major bid and 4+ cards in an undisclosed minor. If weak, responder can pass or pre-empt in the major or, if short in the major, bid 3♣, which opener will pass with clubs or correct to 3◇ with diamonds. If strong, responder bids 2NT as an inquiry bid and opener shows the minor suit held. If responder then bids three of opener's major, that invites game in the major. A rebid by responder in a new suit is forcing.

## Incorporating Acol-Twos in the 2♣ opening

This scheme allows you to include an Acol-Two 1-suited hand within the 2♣ opening. After 2♣ : 2◇ (negative or waiting):

2♡ = artificial, any game-force without 5+ spades.

2♠ = natural game-force with spades as the primary suit. Further bidding is natural.

2NT = 23-24 balanced. Not forcing. Continue as after a 2NT opening bid.

3♣ / 3◇ / 3♡ / 3♠ = Acol-Two with 6+ in the suit bid.

After the 2♡ rebid, responder can make a natural bid with 5-7 points or bid 2♠ as a second negative. With no convenient, natural rebid, responder can also bid 2♠ as a waiting bid. After 2♣ : 2◇, 2♡ : 2♠, opener continues as follows:

2NT = 25+ balanced, forcing to game. Further bidding is the same as after a 2NT opening. Having a 2NT rebid forcing to game is a boon for accurate game investigation.

3♣ / 3◇ / 3♡ = natural, 5+ suit. Further bidding is natural and will continue to at least game.

# What makes a slam?

Successful slam bidding depends on the recognition of two vital factors, namely, power and controls.

**Power:** The means of generating the required number of tricks must be present in one form or another. On balanced hands the power takes the form of points. You normally need 33-34 points in the combined hands for a good chance for twelve tricks at no-trumps, 37 points for thirteen tricks, if the hands are balanced.

Power may also take the form of playing tricks. When there·are long suits about, or when there is a good trump fit and shortages in both hands, slam may be made with considerably less than the normal quota of points.

**Controls:** The combined hands must also possess the controls to ensure that the defenders cannot cash two tricks at once. The minimum requirement for a small slam is first-round control (ace or void) in three suits and second-round control (king or singleton) in the fourth. For a grand slam, first-round control in all suits is needed.

**The trump fit:** Length is not the only criterion for the trump suit in a slam contract. The suit must also be solid or nearly so. In a small slam a loser in the trump suit may be permissible but only if there is no loser outside.

## Direct slam tries

A voluntary bid beyond game by either partner invites slam.

| OPENER | RESPONDER |
|--------|-----------|
| 2NT | 4NT |

Bidding no-trump slams on balanced hands is a matter of arithmetic. With 2NT as 20-22, 4NT shows about 12 points and opener is invited to proceed to 6NT with better than a minimum count.

| OPENER | RESPONDER |
|--------|-----------|
| 2♣ | 2NT |
| 3♠ | 4♠ |
| 5♠ | |

In this case opener's 5♠ is asking about partner's trump holding. Responder is asked to bid slam if holding one of the three top trump honours or better.

50

# Cue-bidding

Once a trump suit has been agreed, the presence of the controls necessary for slam may be confirmed by cue-bidding. The bid of any new suit at a level that commits the partnership to game can be utilised as a cue-bid, denoting first-round control of that suit (via the ace or a void).

| OPENER | RESPONDER |
|--------|-----------|
| 1♠ | 3♠ |
| 4♦ | |

The jump to 3♠ was not forcing but by bidding on over the double jump raise, the opener commits the partnership to game. The bid of 4♦ is therefore a slam try, showing first-round control in diamonds (and not indicating a diamond suit at all). Since it is normal practice to bid the cheapest first-round control, the 4♦ bid simultaneously denies the ace of clubs or a club void. Responder should cue-bid in hearts or clubs, if possible, or otherwise sign off in 4♠.

| OPENER | RESPONDER |
|--------|-----------|
| 1♦ | 2♥ |
| 3♥ | 3♠ |

Hearts have been agreed as trumps and the partnership is committed to game. 3♠ is therefore a cue-bid, showing first-round control in spades.

Do not confuse cue-bids with trial bids.

| OPENER | RESPONDER |
|--------|-----------|
| 1♥ | 2♥ |
| 3♣ | |

In this case the bidding may yet stop below game. 3♣ is not a cue-bid but a try for game, seeking help in clubs.

When first-round control has been shown by a cue-bid, a subsequent bid in the same suit by either partner indicates possession of second-round control (king or singleton).

| OPENER | RESPONDER |
|--------|-----------|
| 2♥ | 3♥ |
| 3♠ | 4♣ |
| 4♦ | 4♠ |

After the Acol-Two opening, hearts are agreed as trumps on the first round. The subsequent bids of 3♠, 4♣ and 4♦ are all cue-bids, affirming first-round control of these suits. The responder's next bid of 4♠ is a further slam try, indicating second-round control in spades, either via the ♠K or a singleton in spades.

# The Blackwood convention

On certain hands it is convenient to check on controls in bulk. The Blackwood 4NT convention can be useful in keeping you out of slam when two aces are missing.

A jump to 4NT after a suit bid from partner, or any bid of 4NT after trumps have been agreed, is a conventional inquiry about the number of aces held. The responses are as follows:

5♣ = no ace or all four aces.
5♦ = one ace.
5♥ = two aces.
5♠ = three aces.

A subsequent bid of 5NT by the 4NT bidder guarantees that all aces are held and is a grand slam try. Partner may bid the grand slam if able to count thirteen tricks. Otherwise partner is expected to show the number of kings held, as follows:

6♣ = no king, 6♦ = one king, 6♥ = two kings,
6♠ = three kings and 6NT = four kings.

### When 4NT is not Blackwood

A bid of 4NT is natural and non-forcing (a) when it is a raise of partner's no-trump bid, and (b) when it is a sign-off by a player who has previously bid no-trumps.

| OPENER | RESPONDER | |
|---|---|---|
| 2♣ | 2♠ | Responder's raise to 4NT is natural, showing a balanced 9 count. Opener |
| 2NT | 4NT | may pass if minimum. |

| OPENER | RESPONDER | |
|---|---|---|
| 1♥ | 2♦ | Again 4NT is natural, non-forcing, inviting slam. Opener should pass if |
| 3NT | 4NT | minimum or bid on with anything more. |

| OPENER | RESPONDER | |
|---|---|---|
| 2NT | 3♣ | No trump suit has been agreed. |
| 3♥ | 3♠ | Opener's 4NT simply denies club |
| 3NT | 4♣ | support. Responder may pass or press |
| 4NT | | on, depending on the values held. |

# Gerber over No-Trumps

Many players adopt this convention to solve the problem of asking for aces when partner opens the bidding in no-trumps.

Using this method, a jump to 4♣ after an opening no-trump bid asks for aces in a manner akin to Blackwood. The answers are:

4♦ = no ace or all four aces.
4♥ = one ace.
4♠ = two aces.
4NT = three aces.

Either 4NT (if available) or 5♣ is then used to ask for kings.

# Roman Key-Card Blackwood (RKCB)

A check on aces can be useful, but on many hands there is a need to find out about the king and queen of trumps as well. This variation of Blackwood, which is increasingly popular among tournament players, enables you to do that. The four aces and the king of trumps are regarded as 'key cards'. When a trump suit has been agreed, either directly or by inference, a bid of 4NT asks partner to respond according to this schedule:

5♣ = 0 or 3 key cards.
5♦ = 1 or 4 key cards.
5♥ = 2 or 5 key cards without the queen of trumps.
5♠ = 2 or 5 key cards with the trump queen as well.

If no trump has suit has been agreed, 4NT refers to the last mentioned suit. For example, 1♠ : 2♥, 4NT asks partner to respond, based on hearts as trumps.

There is no need to worry over the apparent ambiguity of the responses to RKCB. You will be able to tell, by referring to the previous bidding, whether partner is showing the lower or the higher number of key cards.

After a 5♣ or 5♦ response, the 4NT bidder may still be uncertain about the queen of trumps. The next suit (other than trumps) inquires about this card.

## Roman Key-Card Blackwood (RKCB) *continued*

| OPENER | RESPONDER |
|--------|-----------|
| 1♡ | 1♠ |
| 3♠ | 4NT |
| 5♣ | 5◇ |

Having used RKCB and heard 5♣ from partner, responder can be confident that this shows three key cards. 5◇ now asks about the queen of trumps. Lacking the ♠Q opener makes the cheapest bid (5♡). With the ♠Q and no side kings, make the next cheapest bid (5♠). With the ♠Q and one or more kings, opener bids the cheapest king (6♣, 6◇ or 6♡, as the case may be).

If the 4NT bidder holds the trump queen or knows about it from a 5♡ or 5♠ response and is still interested in a grand slam, 5NT is available to ask for kings outside trumps. Partner bids 6♣ (0), 6◇ (1), 6♡ (2) or 6♠ (all three).

### Grand slam force

This is a method of checking on trump solidity for a grand slam. It should be used only where there are no losers outside the trump suit.

A bid of 5NT (not preceded by 4NT) asks partner, 'How many of the top three trump honours (A, K or Q) do you hold?' A simple scheme is to bid seven with two top honours and to sign off in six of the agreed suit with fewer than two. This does not help if you need to know whether partner has all three trump honours or if you need only one trump honour. A simple and effective scheme: Bid 6♣ with 0, 6◇ with 1, 6♡ with 2, 6♠ with all 3.

Opener bids 1NT (12-14) and raises your 3♡ response to 4♡.

♠: --- ♡: Q J 8 7 5 3 ◇: A K Q 8 3 ♣: A K    Bid 5NT.

You certainly want to be in 7♡ if partner has the ♡A and ♡K.

If no trump suit has been set, 5NT refers to the last bid suit.

Partner opens 4♠:

♠: 9 7 6 ♡: A 8 5 3 ◇: --- ♣: A K Q 5 3 2    Bid 5NT.

Opposite ♠A-K-Q-x-x-x-x you want to be in 7♠. Facing a weaker trump suit, 6♠ is enough.

# Opening bids of more than two

Opening bids of three and four (or five of a minor) are made on weak hands containing long, strong suits. The intention is to shut the opponents out of the bidding.

A pre-emptive bid denies the high-card strength to open with a bid of one in a suit. The point range is generally from 3 to 9, but more important than the point count is the number of playing tricks in the hand. It is reasonable to concede a penalty of up to 500 in order to prevent the opponents from making a game. To ensure that the penalty does not exceed 500 when the opponents double, the pre-emptive bidder should be within two tricks of the contract if vulnerable and within three tricks if not vulnerable. The hand should not contain a 4-card major.

**An opening three-bid**
Promises seven playing tricks (6 losers) if vulnerable,
              six playing tricks (7 losers) if not vulnerable.

**An opening four-bid**
Promises eight playing tricks (5 losers) if vulnerable,
              seven playing tricks (6 losers) if not vulnerable.

**An opening 5♣ or 5♢ bid**
Promises nine playing tricks (4 losers) if vulnerable,
              eight playing tricks (5 losers) if not vulnerable.

At tournament bridge, when not vulnerable against vulnerable, the playing tricks required above can be shaded by one.

♠: A Q 10 8 7 4 2  ♡: 5  ♢: 8 6 5  ♣: 9 2   6 playing tricks.
Open 3♠ if not vulnerable, Pass if vulnerable.

♠: 8  ♡: K Q J 9 6 5 2  ♢: Q J 5  ♣: 7 3   7 playing tricks.
Open 4♡ if not vulnerable, 3♡ if vulnerable.

♠: K J 10 9 7 5 3 2  ♡: 4  ♢: 8  ♣: K J 10  8 playing tricks.
Open 4♠ vulnerable or not.

♠: 2  ♡: 9  ♢: A K J 9 7 6 5 4 2  ♣: 4 3   9 playing tricks.
Open 5♢ vulnerable or not.

## Responding to pre-emptive bids

Raise an opening three-bid with more than two winners if vulnerable, with more than three winners if not vulnerable. Be conservative in counting winners. The quick trick scale (page 11) is a good guide. Aces are most valuable and a K-Q holding may be of no use opposite a singleton. Trump support is not critical since opener's suit should be long and strong.

♠: 5   ♡: A 7 3   ◇: A K 8 5   ♣: 10 8 7 6 2
Raise 3♠ to 4♠ if vulnerable but pass if not vulnerable.
Raise 3♡ to 4♡ whether vulnerable or not.

♠: A K 8 7   ♡: 6   ◇: A Q 9 8 3   ♣: 7 3 2
Raise 3♣ to 5♣ whether vulnerable or not.

**A response of 3NT** promises a balanced hand with good stoppers in the other suits and preferably honours in opener's suit.

♠: A 10 6   ♡: K Q 8   ◇: J 10 4 2   ♣: A Q 6
Respond 3NT to an opening three-bid in any suit.

**A response in a new suit** is forcing below game and suggests an alternative game contract.

♠: A Q J 8 7 3   ♡: 2   ◇: A K 5   ♣: 10 6 5
Respond 3♠ to an opening bid of 3♣, 3◇ or 3♡.

## The gambling 3NT

The opening bid of 3NT is made on a hand containing a solid 7-card minor and not more than a queen in outside strength.

♠: 8   ♡: 7 3   ◇: A K Q 10 7 4 2   ♣: Q 4 3
Open 3NT whether vulnerable or not.

Having opened 3NT, leave further action to partner who can choose to play in no-trumps or in opener's suit.

♠: Q J 7 4   ♡: A K 6 2   ◇: Q 10 4   ♣: 8 3   Pass 3NT.

♠: 7 6 5   ♡: K Q 10 9 5   ◇: 9 7 5   ♣: 8 6   Bid 4♣.
Opener will correct to 4◇ if that is the long suit.

♠: 8   ♡: A J 9 6 5   ◇: 8 7 3   ♣: A Q 5 3   Bid 5◇.

# Defensive bidding

Half the time it will be the opponents who open the bidding. If you wish to compete you have a number of options.

## Overcalls

A minimum overcall of one or two in a suit may be made on a hand that lacks the high-card requirements for an opening bid, but it must be strong in playing tricks. After an opening bid on your right, your left-hand opponent will be eager to penalise an injudicious overcall. To protect yourself against a costly penalty you should be within two tricks of your contract if vulnerable and within three if not vulnerable. Requirements:

AT THE 1-LEVEL

a) 8-15 points.
b) A good 5-card or longer suit (or a powerful 4-card suit).
c) 5 playing tricks (8 losers) if vulnerable, 4 playing tricks (9 losers) if not vulnerable.

AT THE 2-LEVEL

a) 10-15 points.
b) A good 5-card or longer suit (never a 4-card suit).
c) 6 playing tricks ( 7 losers) if vulnerable, 5 playing tricks (8 losers) if not vulnerable.

The upper limit for an overcall is 7 playing tricks. With 8 playing tricks (5 losers) or better, start with a double and bid your suit on the next round (5 losers) or make a jump-bid in your suit (4 losers) on the next round.

## The suit quality test

An overcall requires high card strength and suit quality. To see whether your suit is adequate for an overcall, add the number of cards in the suit to the number of honour cards in the suit. Count the jack and ten as honours here only if you also hold a higher honour. If the total equals or exceeds the number of tricks for which you are bidding, your suit quality is fine.

| SUIT | QUALITY | NOTES |
|---|---|---|
| K-Q-7-6-3 | 7 | Fine for a 1-level overcall, not 2-level. |
| K-Q-J-6 | 7 | Fine for a 1-level overcall, not 2-level. |
| A-Q-J-8-3 | 8 | Fine for a 1-level or 2-level overcall. |
| Q-8-7-4-2 | 6 | Too weak for an overcall at any level. |

## Defensive bidding

**Responding to overcalls**

| POINTS | ACTION |
|---|---|
| **6 *or less*** | Generally pass, but give a single raise with values for a raise of an opening bid. |
| **7-10** | a) Give a single raise with trump support. |
| | b) Bid a good suit of your own at the 1-level. |
| | c) Bid 1NT with a stopper in their suit. |
| **11-14** | a) Give a double raise with trump support. |
| | b) Bid a good suit of your own. |
| | c) Bid 2NT with a balanced hand and at least one stopper in their suit. |
| **15 *or more*** | a) Raise the major suit to game with trump support. |
| | b) Bid a good suit of your own. |
| | c) Bid 3NT (15-17) with a balanced hand and at least one stopper in their suit. |
| | d) Jump-bid a good suit of your own. |
| | e) Bid the opponent's suit (forcing for one round). |

The above is a standard approach to overcalls. Recommended is to play change of suit forcing in reply to an overcall. In the modern style jump-raises of overcalls are played as pre-emptive and strong supporting hands start by bidding the enemy suit. Suppose the bidding has started:

| W | N | E | S |
|---|---|---|---|
| 1♦ | 1♠ | No | ? |

2♠ = 6-9 points with 3-card support.
3♠ = below 10 points, 4+ support, usually 8 losers.
4♠ = below 10 points, 4+ support, usually 7 losers.
2♦ = 10+ points and 3-card support.
3♦ = 10+ points and 4+ support.

After 2♦, overcaller's repeat of the suit (2♠ here) is weak. Pass with 10-13 points, raise to three with 14-15 points.

After 3♦, overcaller's repeat of the suit (3♠ here) is weak. Pass with 7-8 losers, raise to game with 6 losers or fewer.

# Defensive bidding *continued*

### The 1NT overcall

Whether the opening bid of 1NT is weak or strong, the 1NT overcall is always strong (commonly 15-17, but many players prefer 15-18 or even 16-18). The 1NT overcall indicates a balanced hand with at least one stopper in the enemy suit.

The advancer (partner of the overcaller) passes, raises, signs off at the 2-level, uses 2♣ Stayman, and so on, as for a 1NT opening but with 3 points less than for a weak 1NT. Play the bid of the enemy suit as a good hand with a shortage in their suit.

### The strong jump-overcall

This shows a good hand with a strong 6+ suit. The point range is about 14-17 and usually 7-8 playing tricks (5-6 losers). Suppose right-hand opponent opens 1♡.

| | | | | |
|---|---|---|---|---|
| ♠: A Q J 9 8 3 | ♡: 7 3 | ◇: A K 6 | ♣: 8 4 | Bid 2♠. |
| ♠: A Q | ♡: 6 | ◇: A 8 2 | ♣: K Q J 7 6 4 2 | Bid 3♣. |

### Advancer's actions after a strong jump-overcall

| POINTS | ACTION |
|---|---|
| **5** *or less* | Generally pass, but give a single raise with three trumps and better than one trick. |
| **6-9** | a) Raise with 2+ trumps.<br>b) Bid NT with a sure stopper in the enemy suit.<br>c) Bid a good 5+ suit of your own. |
| **10** *or more* | a) Raise to game with trump support.<br>b) Bid 3NT with a sure stopper in the enemy suit.<br>c) Bid the opponent's suit (forcing to game). |

**Intermediate jump-overcalls:** These show a good 6+ suit and 11-14 points. Add 3 points to the above ranges for advancer's action after an intermediate jump-overcall.

**Weak jump-overcalls:** Show a good 6+ suit and 6-10 points. Add 8 points to the above ranges for advancer's action.

# Defensive bidding *continued*

## The unusual 2NT

After an enemy opening it is not useful to use a 2NT overcall to show a balanced 20-22 points. Such a powerful holding is very rare and can be easily described after starting with a take-out double. The 2NT overcall after a 1-opening has come to be used to show a two-suiter. After their 1♡ or 1♠ opening, the 2NT overcall shows at least 5-5 in the minors and a weak hand, normally around 8-12 points. With a 6-5 or 6-6 pattern, or at favourable vulnerability, the point count can be reduced.

The suits should be strong (five honours between the two suits is a reasonable holding). As 2NT suggests a sacrifice to partner avoid bidding it with 13+ points or more than two quick tricks. After a minor suit opening, 2NT is commonly played as a 5-5 hand with hearts and the other minor.

Right-hand opponent opens 1♡.

| ♠: J 3 | ♡: 5 | ◇: K Q 9 8 3 | ♣: Q J 10 9 2 | Bid 2NT. |
| ♠: J 3 | ♡: 5 | ◇: A 7 6 3 2 | ♣: A 7 5 4 3 | Pass. |

The suits are too weak for 2NT and neither suit has sufficient quality for a 2-level overcall. There is no shame in passing.

### Advancer's actions after the unusual 2NT

If weak, bid your longer minor. With equal length, bid the stronger. If third hand doubles, pass with equal length and let partner choose the minor. With little defence and an excellent fit with one minor (4-card or better support) and a singleton, void or a top honour doubleton in the other minor, be prepared to sacrifice in 5-minor. Do not sacrifice if balanced or with more than two defensive tricks.

The jump to 4-minor is pre-emptive, not constructive. With a strong hand, advancer can bid the other major (6+ suit), seeking doubleton support, or bid the enemy suit.

After (1♡) : 2NT : (No) to you –

| ♠: A 9 2 | ♡: J 7 6 4 3 | ◇: 9 8 3 | ♣: K 2 | Bid 3◇. |
| ♠: A K | ♡: 9 8 7 4 2 | ◇: 6 | ♣: K 7 5 4 3 | Bid 5♣. |

# Defensive bidding *continued*

### Bidding the enemy suit

Traditionally this has shown a powerful two-suited or three-suited hand, short in the enemy suit and with values close to game. It is forcing until suit agreement has been reached. Advancer bids the cheapest 4-card unbid suit and awaits to hear from partner.

Right-hand opponent opens 1♡.

♠: A K J 10 3   ♡: 4   ◇: A Q 8 7 5 3   ♣: A      Bid 2♡.

Such strong use of the enemy suit has lost support, especially among tournament players, because such hands are very rare and you can achieve the same position by starting with a take-out double and bidding the enemy suit after partner's reply. The popular use of the enemy suit nowadays is to show a two-suiter, at least 5-5, known as the Michaels Cue-Bid convention.

### Michaels Cue-Bid

*After a major suit opening:*

(1♡): 2♡  = 5+ spades and a 5+ minor.
(1♠): 2♠  = 5+ hearts and a 5+ minor.

It is sensible to regard the Michaels Cue-Bid as the Unusual 2NT except that the suits are not the minors.

### Advancer's actions after a Michaels Cue-Bid

If weak, support partner's major if possible. Without support, bid 3♣. Partner passes with clubs, bids 3◇ with diamonds.

If strong, jump to game in partner's major or bid 2NT, showing at least game-inviting values and asking partner to disclose the minor. 2NT and then reverting to the major invites game.

*After a minor suit opening:*

(1♣): 2♣ or (1◇): 2◇ = both majors, at least 5-5. In reply, support a major if possible. If strong, bid game or bid their suit or use the 2NT inquiry to which partner bids 3♣ minimum and 5-5, 3◇ maximum and 5-5, 3♡ = 6 hearts, 3♠ = 6 spades.

## The take-out double

This is a conventional way to ask for partner's best suit. It is vital to be able to distinguish a take-out double from a penalty double since the take-out double says, 'Please bid' and the penalty double says, 'Please pass'. According to traditional rules a double is intended for take-out only if:

a) It is a double of a suit bid and made at the first opportunity.
b) It is a double of a suit not higher than the 3-level.
c) The doubler's partner has not bid or doubled.

These rules have all been whittled away in modern times.

| W | N | E | S | |
|---|---|---|---|---|
| 1◇ | 1♠ | No | No | North's double is not at the first opportunity but it is still meant as |
| 2◇ | Dble | | | a take-out double. |

Doubles of pre-emptive bids are commonly played for take-out, whether the pre-empt is at the three-level or four-level.

| W | N | E | S | |
|---|---|---|---|---|
| 1♠ | No | 4♠ | Dble | South's double is best played as take-out with shortage in spades. |

| W | N | E | S | |
|---|---|---|---|---|
| 1♡ | No | 1NT | Dble | Double of a 1NT opening is for penalties, but double of a 1NT response is used as a take-out |

double of the suit opened. South has a take-out double of 1♡.

| W | N | E | S | |
|---|---|---|---|---|
| 1♡ | 2♣ | Dble | | Double after partner has opened used to be played for penalties. Today the vast majority of players |

(certainly in tournament play) use the double by responder as a take-out double with 6+ points (see Negative Doubles, page 70).

These are sensible guidelines for doubles in the modern era. A double is for take-out:

a) After the opponents have bid and raised a suit.
b) After any pre-emptive action by an opponent, whether it is a pre-emptive opening, overcall or raise.
c) After any suit bid at the 1- or 2-level unless the partnership has stipulated such a double is for penalties.

# The take-out double *continued*

After right-hand opponent opens with a suit bid, a take-out double is possible on a variety of hands. There are three point ranges for such a take-out double, with specific requirements. In general, the lower the point count, the better the shape must be.

**a) 10-15 points:** The doubler's hand should have 3+ support for every unbid suit and have the enemy suit as the shortest suit. To double with 10 points, the hand pattern should be 5-4-4-0 and to double with 11 points it should be 4-4-4-1 or 5-4-4-0.

**b) 16-18 points:** With this strength you may double with any shape other than a hand suitable for a 1NT overcall. Hands too strong for a simple overcall can fall into this area.

**c) 19+ points:** Any shape is acceptable with such strength.

These hands all qualify for a take-out double after a 1♡ opening on your right:

♠:K 7 3 2  ♡:2  ◇:Q J 6  ♣:A K 9 4 3          Type a)
♠:Q 7 6 3  ♡:9  ◇:K Q 7 5  ♣:A 9 5 2          Type a)
♠:A J 8  ♡:9 3  ◇:A K 9 3  ♣:Q J 7 6          Type a)
♠:A K J 7 3  ♡:8 3  ◇:A Q J  ♣:K 4 3          Type b)
♠:A K 5  ♡:8 7 4  ◇:K J 9  ♣:A Q 8 2          Type b)
♠:A K 5  ♡:A Q 7  ◇:Q J 9 4  ♣:K 9 5          Type c)
♠:K Q J 8  ♡:- - -  ◇:A Q J 5  ♣:A K J 8 2    Type c)

If both opponents have bid, a take-out double asks partner to choose one of the unbid suits.

| W | N | E | S | |
|---|---|---|---|---|
| 1◇ | No | 1♠ | Dble | South's double asks North to choose between hearts and clubs. |

South might have: ♠: A 3  ♡: K Q 9 4  ◇: 6 5 3  ♣: A Q J 4.

When opener's suit is raised after your double and the bidding comes back to you, double again if you are strong enough:

| W | N | E | S | |
|---|---|---|---|---|
| 1♡ | Dble | 3♡ | No | With a three-suiter short in hearts, North should double again with |
| No | ? | | | 16 points or more. |

# Responding to a take-out double

When partner makes a take-out double and next player passes, you must find a response no matter how weak your hand. The only exception is if you have four or more playing tricks in the doubled suit. In that case you may pass for penalties.

| POINTS | YOU SHOULD: |
|---|---|
| **0-4** | Bid your longest of the other three suits but prefer a major to a minor, even if the major is shorter. With suits of equal length, choose the stronger. |
| **5-8** | a) Bid a suit, with priority given to a major suit. b) With no major to bid, choose 1NT with a stopper in their suit and a balanced hand. c) Jump in a 5-card major with 7-8 points and a void, singleton or two doubletons. |
| **9-11** | a) Jump in a 4-card or 5-card suit (prefer a major). b) Bid game in a 6-card major. c) With no major, bid 2NT with their suit stopped. |
| **12** *or more* | a) Bid game in a 6-card or strong 5-card major. b) Bid the enemy suit (forcing to suit agreement). c) Bid 3NT with their suit stopped and no major. |

When the next player bids over the double, you are relieved of the duty of finding a response on a weak hand. Pass with 0-4 points, but bid with 5 points or more and jump-bid with 9 or more.

| W | N | E | S |
|---|---|---|---|
| 1♠ | Dble | 1NT | ? |

♠: 8 4 3   ♡: A J 7 6 5   ◇: 9 4 3 2   ♣: 5   Bid 2♡. With an extra ace, South should jump to 3♡.

## Pre-emptive overcalls

When an opponent has opened, a double jump-bid in a new suit is pre-emptive in nature like an opening bid of three or four in a suit. As usual, the overcaller should be within two tricks of the bid if vulnerable and within three if not vulnerable.

# Re-opening the bidding

When an opening of one in a suit is followed by two passes, it is usually safe for the fourth player to assume that partner has some values. There are strong hands that are unsuited to immediate action in the second seat, especially with length in opener's suit. Partner could easily have 13 or more points.

In the pass-out seat, protect your partner's pass by overcalling or doubling on shaded values. Re-opening the bidding in this position is known as protecting or balancing.

**Overcalls:** A re-opening overcall may be made with 7 points. There is no suit quality requirement for a re-opening overcall. After an opening bid of 1♡ and two passes, be prepared to bid 1♠ with ♠: J 10 7 6 2   ♡: 8 4   ◇: A K 6   ♣: 7 4 3.

**Jump-overcalls:** These show 12-15 points and good 6+ suit. After an opening bid of 1◇ and two passes, bid 2♡ with: ♠: 9 5 4   ♡: A Q J 8 5 2   ◇: 7   ♣: A J 3.

**1NT:** In the pass-out seat 1NT shows a balanced 11-14 points. If stronger and balanced, double first and then bid no-trumps.

**Double:** A balancing double may be made on as few as 8 points when the shape is good.
After an opening bid of 1♡ and two passes, double with:
♠: J 10 8 4   ♡: 8   ◇: A 8 3 2   ♣: K 7 6 5.
With length and strength in hearts, partner may convert your take-out double into penalties by passing.

## When the opponents intervene

Overcalls and take-out doubles can have an effect on the responses and rebids of the opening side.

### 1) Responses

When partner's opening bid is overcalled by your right-hand opponent you need not strain to bid. Partner is assured of another bid. The meaning of your bids does not change but a bid in no-trumps must include at least one stopper in their suit.

# When the opponents intervene *continued*

With any strong hand, make your normal response. Consider playing for penalties (see pages 67-68) with length and strength in their suit and shortage in partner's suit. You can also bid the enemy suit to show game-going values with no clear direction or with support for opener's suit.

If your right-hand opponent doubles partner's opening bid of one in a suit, raise pre-emptively to make it more difficult for the fourth player to enter the auction.

**A single raise** can be made on 3 or 4 points with trump support and a ruffing value.

**A double raise** can be made below 10 points with four trumps and 8 losers.

**A 2NT response** shows 10+ points and 4+ trumps. If minimum, opener rebids 3-in-the-suit-opened. With more, bid game.

**A redouble** shows 10 or more points, denies support for opener's suit and is looking for penalties. It is normally strong in at least two of the unbid suits. After a redouble, a double by either partner is for penalties.

Other actions have their normal meaning, a new suit is forcing, but a jump-bid in a new suit is used to show about 6-8 points and a good 6-card suit.

## 2) **Opener's rebids**

When the left-hand opponent overcalls and partner passes, opener may pass with length and strength in the overcalled suit. Otherwise opener should re-open, even with modest values and particularly so if short in the overcalled suit. Opener's options:

a) Double for take-out with shortage in the enemy suit.
b) Bid a new 5-card suit.
c) Rebid a good 6-card suit.
d) Rebid 1NT with 17-19 points and a stopper in their suit.

If partner has responded and fourth player doubles, opener should rebid normally but redouble with a balanced 16 or more points.

# Penalty doubles

A double is for penalties and not intended to be taken out in the following cases:

a) After a previous penalty double or penalty pass.
b) A double of a no-trump opening or a no-trump overcall.
c) After partner's two-level opening.
d) After any pre-emptive bid by partner.
e) After a strength-showing redouble by either partner.
f) A double of their artificial bid.
g) When the doubler had an earlier chance to make a take-out double of the suit and failed to do so.
h) Whenever the partnership has stipulated that the double should be for penalties.

## When to play for penalties

Double a no-trump contract when your point count indicates that the opponents have overbid or after their invitational auction when you can tell that their suits are breaking badly.

Play for penalties against a suit contract when your quick tricks plus your trump tricks indicate that they should be two down at least. To double a low-level suit contract, you should have strength in their suit and shortage in partner's suit.

Accept any penalty rather than bid a doubtful game, but if game is sure for your side, double only if the likely penalty exceeds the value of your game. Count only sure winners in defence when penalising a suit contract. Count A-Q as two winners if the suit has been bid on your right, but as one winner if the suit is bid on your left. Discount a holding such as K-x or K-x-x if the suit has been bid on your left.

Rely on partner for two defensive tricks for an opening bid, for one trick for a minimum response or an overcall. Do not be eager for penalties when you have length in partner's suit. Count a holding such as A-K-x-x-x as only one trick if partner has supported the suit.

# Penalty doubles *continued*

## Penalising an overcall

Juicy penalties can be obtained when they overcall at the 2-level. Great length in trumps is not necessary, but you should have four or five trumps, including at least two winners in the trump suit. For a successful low-level penalty of a suit bid, you should be short in partner's suit and your side should have at least 20 points in the combined hands.

Partner opens 1♡, next player overcalls 2♣ or 2♢. You have:
♠: K 8 3   ♡: 10   ♢: A Q 7 2   ♣: J 9 7 5 3   Go for penalties.

## Doubling a 1NT overcall

When partner opens with a bid of one in a suit and the next player overcalls 1NT, double with 10 points or more. Any raise or a suit response at the two-level shows a weak hand.

## Doubling a 1NT opening

When your right-hand opponent opens 1NT you cannot afford to delay if you have a good hand. You should double a weak 1NT for penalties with 15 points or more. You should also have a good suit to lead. With a very shapely hand it is better to compete than to double if your long suit is not solid. Against a strong 1NT, you need 17 points or more to double for penalties.

The doubler's partner should pass on all balanced hands. If strong, expect a good penalty. If weak, hope for the best. With a weak, unbalanced hand, take the double out into a 5+ suit. With a strong, unbalanced hand, you may opt for game rather than a penalty by jumping to the 3-level or bidding 2NT, forcing.

## When partner's 1NT is doubled

Do not let the doubler off the hook if your side has the balance of power. Redouble with 10 or more points opposite a weak 1NT, with 7 or more opposite a strong 1NT. Thereafter all doubles are for penalties. If they remove to a suit, be prepared to double with any decent 4-card holding in their suit.

# Doubling for a lead

There are situations where a double requests a specific lead.

## 1) **Double of 3NT**

When a contract of 3NT is doubled by the defender not on lead, the opening leader is expected to follow this list of priorities:

a) If just one suit has been bid by the defenders, lead that suit.
b) If both defender's have bid a suit, the double calls for the opening leader's suit.
c) If neither defender has bid a suit, lead dummy's suit.
d) If no suit has been bid, e.g., 1NT : 3NT, some play that the double asks for a spade lead. That is better than no agreement.

## 2) **The Lightner double**

If the opponents have bid freely to slam (not a sacrifice), the double by the defender not on lead asks for an unusual lead. The opening leader is directed not to lead trumps or an unbid suit or any suit bid by the defenders. Top priority is the first suit bid by dummy. If dummy has bid no suit other than trumps, the doubler has a void and asks you to find it. Many pairs extend this rule to game contracts if it is clear that the doubler cannot have a genuine penalty double, such as by a pre-emptive opener.

## 3) **Doubling artificial bids**

The double of an artificial bid usually asks partner to lead that suit. Doubles of replies to Blackwood, cue-bids, fourth-suit and other artificial bids are primarily lead-directing.

### Exceptions

After a weak 1NT opening by an opponent and a 2♣ Stayman reply or a transfer response, double is used to say, 'I have a strong hand and I would have doubled 1NT for penalties'. After a strong 1NT, double of an artificial reply is lead-directing.

Many pairs play that the double of a splinter bid asks for a specific lead, not of the splinter suit (singleton or void) but of the higher-ranking suit excluding trumps and the splinter suit.

# Negative doubles

After an opening bid of one in a suit and a suit overcall, the double by responder has been abandoned as a penalty double by almost all tournament players. Instead, responder's double is played for take-out with the emphasis on any unbid major suit. Such a double by responder is called a 'negative double'.

The strength promised is 6 points or more for a negative double at the 1- or 2-level if this does not push the partnership beyond the 2-level. If the double commits the partnership to the 3-level but below 3NT, 9 points or more would be expected, and 12 points or more if the double might commit the partnership to 3NT or the 4-level or higher.

## Suits promised

*No major has been bid:* After auctions such as 1♣ : (1◇) or 1◇ : (2♣) or 1♣ : (2◇) or 1♣ : (3◇) or 1◇ : (3♣) the negative double promises both majors, at least 4 cards in each.

*Only one major has been bid:* After 1♣ : (1♠) or 1◇ : (2♡) or similar auctions, the negative double promises 4+ cards in the other major. Specifically, 1♣ : (1♡) : Double shows four spades, while a 1♠ response over 1♡ would show five spades. For 1◇: (2♡) : 2♠ responder is showing 5+ spades and 10+ points, while the double could be 5+ spades and 6-9 points (too weak for 2♠) or 4+ spades and 6+ points (wide-ranging).

The negative double helps to solve common bidding problems when the overcall robs you of your natural bid. Suppose you hold:  ♠: 6 5 4  ♡: A 10 7 5  ◇: Q J 9 4  ♣: 9 6
Partner opens 1♣ and the next player overcalls 1♠. Standard methods provide no way to express your values since you are too weak to come in at the two-level and the lack of a spade stopper precludes 1NT. The negative double shows that you have a hand worth a 1♡ response initially.

*Both majors have been bid:* After 1♡ : (1♠) or 1♠ : (2♡) or similar auctions, a negative double promises both minors, at least 4 cards in each, and denies primary support for opener's major.

Negative doubles *continued*

### Opener's rebids after a negative double

Treat the negative double as a minimum response, 6-9 points, and act accordingly. Make a minimum bid with a minimum opening and a jump-bid with extra values. With enough for game, bid game direct if the right game is obvious or bid the enemy suit to force to game. With 10 points or more, responder will bid again after a minimum rebid by opener.

On rare occasions opener may have a hand with length and strength in the suit overcalled. If so, pass the negative double and play for penalties. Suppose the bidding starts:

| W | N | E | S |
|---|---|---|---|
| 1♠ | 2◇ | Dble | No |

With ♠: A K 8 4 3   ♡: 3   ◇: A J 7 6 2   ♣: 9 3, West passes.

### Re-opening after responder's pass

Playing negative doubles responder will often pass on a hand suitable for penalties (because double would be for takeout).

♠: 8 5   ♡: Q 4   ◇: K 9 8 6   ♣: A J 9 6 3

Suppose partner opens 1♠ and next player overcalls 2♣. You want to double for penalties but this is not possible if you are playing negative doubles. The double would show a different sort of hand, one that included four hearts. To secure penalties, responder passes and awaits a re-opening double by opener. Responder then passes the re-opening double for penalties.

After an overcall is followed by two passes, opener should pass only with length in the enemy suit. With shortage in their suit, be quick to re-open with a double. This double is for take-out. If responder is weak, the double will be taken out in the normal way. With the penalties hand, responder will leave the double in.

After 1♠ : (2◇), passed back to opener:

♠: A J 7 3 2   ♡: Q 4 2   ◇: 6   ♣: K Q 5 4          Double.

♠: A J 7 3 2   ♡: K 4   ◇: K 9 6 3   ♣: Q 5          Pass.

## Part-score competitive strategy

*3-over-2 rule:* If they bid and raise a suit to the 2-level, pass, pass to you, be eager to compete in the pass-out seat.
*3-over-3 rule:* Once the bidding is at the 3-level, bid above them at the 3-level with 9 trumps, pass and defend with 8 trumps.
*4-over-3 rule:* Do not compete to the 4-level on a part-score hand unless your side has 10+ trumps.
*With 9 trumps, compete for 9 tricks.*
*With 10 trumps, compete for 10 tricks.*

## Defence to Weak Two-Bids

Treat their weak two-opening in much the same way as a one-bid, doubling for take-out and overcalling 2NT on balanced hands with 16-18 points. After 2NT, advancer uses the same bidding structure as after a 2NT opening (see page 24).

Simple overcalls are natural and a bid of their suit is a hand too strong for a 3♣ or 3♢ overcall. It asks primarily for partner to bid 3NT with a stopper in their suit. For tournament players, the jumps to 4♣ and 4♢ can be used like the Michaels Cue-Bid, to show 5+ cards in the suit bid and 5 cards in the other major.

## Defence to opening three-bids

The almost universally preferred method is to play double for take-out, with 3NT to play (16+ points, balanced and a stopper in the suit opened) and suit bids as natural. In the direct seat, double shows a hand of 15 points or more and 6 losers or fewer. In reply, partner should bid for game with 9 points or better or bid at the cheapest level if weaker. You may pass the double for penalties with 4+ trumps and two trump winners.

A suit overcall at the 3-level should also have about 6 losers. Bid game in a major with a good 6+ suit and 5 losers. After a pre-empt it is sensible to play partner for two tricks. Bidding the suit opened shows a two-suiter, normally at least 5-5, and about 5 losers. After (3-any) : Pass : Pass, the above requirements can be shaded by three points or by one trick.

# Opening leads against no-trumps

Normal strategy in defending against no-trump contracts is to lead from your longest suit to try to establish the low cards as winners. The card to lead is <u>underlined</u> in the table below.

**Leading from length** (4-card or longer suits)

| HOLDING | NOTES |
|---|---|
| <u>A</u> K Q x<br><u>K</u> Q J x<br><u>Q</u> J 10 x<br><u>J</u> 10 9 x<br><u>10</u> 9 8 x | The most desirable leads against no-trumps are from a sequence of honour cards. The top card is led from a sequence of three or more cards headed by an honour card. |
| <u>A</u> K J x<br><u>K</u> Q 10 x<br><u>Q</u> J 9 x<br><u>J</u> 10 8 x<br><u>10</u> 9 7 x | Almost as good is the lead from a near-sequence where two cards are in sequence followed by a gap of just one card to the next in sequence. To lead top card here, the near-sequence needs to be headed by an honour. |
| A Q <u>J</u> x<br>A Q <u>10</u> 9<br>A <u>J</u> 10 x<br>A <u>10</u> 9 x<br>K <u>J</u> 10 x | Where there is a gap after the top honour in a suit followed by two touching honours or the 10-9, you have an 'interior sequence'. From such a holding, lead the top of the touching cards. |
| K <u>10</u> 9 x<br>Q <u>10</u> 9 x | From A-Q-J-x-x or longer, start with the ace if you have a sure entry in another suit. |
| A Q x <u>x</u><br>A J x <u>x</u><br>K Q x <u>x</u><br>K x x <u>x</u><br>Q J x <u>x</u><br>Q x x <u>x</u><br>J x x x<br>10 x x <u>x</u> | When none of the above sequence combinations is held, the fourth-highest card is led from any holding headed by one or two honour cards.<br>The weaker the suit, the less desirable the lead, but on most hands the lead from a 5+ suit represents the best chance to defeat the contract. With a weak 5+ suit and an entryless hand, try a short suit lead in the hope of hitting partner's long suit. |
| x <u>x</u> x x<br>x x x <u>x</u> x | From a suit lacking an honour, lead second-highest. from a 4-card suit but fourth-highest from a 5+ suit. |

## Opening leads against no-trumps *continued*

### Short suit leads

One logical occasion to lead from shortage is when your partner has bid the suit. Such a lead is particularly attractive if partner has made an overcall or a pre-emptive bid. A short suit lead may also be best (a) when partner is likely to have length in the suit on the bidding, (b) when it is the only unbid suit, or (c) when all your other leads are less attractive. The card to lead is underlined in each case.

*Any doubleton:* Lead the top card but do not lead from a doubleton honour unless partner has bid the suit.

*3-card suit headed by an honour card and the one below it:* Lead the top of the touching cards.

<u>A</u>-K-x, <u>K</u>-Q-x, <u>Q</u>-J-x, <u>J</u>-10-x, <u>10</u>-9-x.

*3-card suit with an interior sequence:* Lead the top of the touching cards.

A-<u>J</u>-10, A-<u>10</u>-9, K-<u>J</u>-10, K-<u>10</u>-9, Q-<u>10</u>-9.

*3-card suit with one honour or two non-touching honours* Lead the bottom card.

A-J-<u>x</u>, A-10-<u>x</u>, K-J-<u>x</u>, K-10-<u>x</u>, Q-10-<u>x</u>, A-x-<u>x</u>, K-x-<u>x</u>, Q-x-<u>x</u>, J-x-<u>x</u>, 10-x-<u>x</u>.

A-<u>Q</u>-x   A special case. You need to unblock the suit. To lead the ace would not be wrong but the queen is usually better.

*3-card suit with no honour:*
x-<u>x</u>-x   Lead middle and play the top card next (middle-up-down) but lead top if you have shown 3+ cards in the bidding.

### Asking partner to unblock

If partner leads an honour card from a long suit and you hold the honour below, you are asked to play it. Lead the honour above the missing honour from 4-card or longer sequences like:
A-<u>K</u>-J-10-x, A-K-<u>Q</u>-10-x or K-Q-10-9-x

# Leads against suit contracts

When leading against a suit contract you do not normally expect to be able to establish a long suit. A long suit lead is not as attractive as against no-trumps since declarer will be able to control your suit by ruffing. The emphasis is more on safety, particularly at game-level. Try to find a lead that will not give away a trick. Usually best is the top card from a 3-card or longer honour sequence or the ace from a suit headed by the A-K.

The leads against suit contracts are the same as for leads against no-trumps with two important exceptions:

*Do not lead low from a suit headed by the ace.* Lead the ace.

*Do not lead low from a suit headed by the K-Q.* Lead the king.

While leading from a suit headed by the A-K appeals greatly, leading from a suit headed by the ace without the king is a risky proposition. Much of the time such a lead sets up winners for declarer. Retain the ace to capture one of declarer's honours.

*Rule 1:* Do not lead from a suit headed by the A without the K.

*Rule 2:* If you must break Rule 1, lead the ace, not a low card.

## Special cases

### A-K and A-K-x(-x-x)

It is important to distinguish A-K doubleton from a 3-card or longer suit headed by the A-K. As you lead the ace from A-K-x or longer, start with the king from A-K doubleton and play the ace next. This should make partner aware that you have led a doubleton and partner should give a suit-preference signal on the king to indicate which suit you should play next.

### Q-J-x-x and J-10-x-x

It is normal to lead fourth-highest from these holdings. To lead an honour can be costly if it collides with a singleton honour or two honours doubleton with partner. If partner is known to have length in the suit, leading the top card becomes preferable.

# Leads against suit contracts *continued*

## Short suit leads

From three or four cards with no honour card, the most popular is to start with the second-highest card and play the top card next. This distinguishes such holdings from a doubleton, where the sequence of play is high-then-lower. However, if you are known to have more than a doubleton in the suit (perhaps you raised partner's suit), by all means lead the top from three or four rags to let partner know you have no honour card in the suit.

The lead from three or four low cards in an unbid suit is passive and safe most of the time. The worst that can happen is that you locate a queen for declarer, who might have guessed right anyway. This is the lead to choose when you fear that a lead from any other suit might give away a trick.

A doubleton lead has better attacking prospects for you may be able to score a third-round ruff. This becomes more attractive when you have a quick entry in trumps such as A-x or K-x-x. That may enable you to gain the lead early in trumps and obtain a ruff with one of your worthless trumps. A doubleton lead is likely to be successful in the same circumstances that make a singleton lead attractive, i.e., when your hand is weak.

The lead of a singleton can be most dynamic on the right kind of hand. If partner has the ace you will be able to obtain an immediate ruff and you may be able to achieve more than one ruff if you find partner with another quick entry. The drawback to a singleton lead is that it may ruin partner's holding in the suit. For this reason a singleton should not be led unless there is a real chance of scoring a ruff. The weaker the hand, the better the prospects for a singleton lead, particularly if you have trump control with A-x, A-x-x or K-x-x. Do not lead a singleton if you are very strong, for it is unlikely that partner will have an entry. Suspect partner's lead to be a singleton if the lead is in a suit bid by dummy *or* partner has pre-empted and leads a suit other than the long suit *or* your side has bid and raised a suit and partner leads some other suit.

76

# Leads against suit contracts *continued*

## When to lead trumps

A trump may be chosen as a passive lead from two or three rags when you fear that anything else will give away a trick, but it can be a devastating attacking lead when the bidding indicates the need to cut down dummy's ruffing power. Lead a trump in the following situations:

a) When you are strong in declarer's second suit.
b) When you suspect declarer will play a cross-ruff. This can occur when they have bid two suits and play in their third suit.
c) When they are in a 4-4 fit and you have five rag trumps.
d) When declarer, having been supported, tries no-trumps and dummy reverts to the trump suit (thus showing ruffing power).
e) When your side has strength in all three suits outside trumps.
f) When declarer is known to have a 4-4-4-1 or 5-4-4-0 pattern.
g) When the opponents are sacrificing.
h) When your take-out double is passed for penalties.

It is standard to lead bottom from an even number of trumps and middle-down-up with an odd number. If a trump lead is indicated do not be afraid to lead away from an honour card. A trick given away by the lead is likely to come back with interest.

A trump lead is not usually a good idea if dummy has not supported the suit or when you have a singleton trump, except in case h) above, or when you have four trumps.

## Forcing defence

If you have four trumps or feel partner probably has four trumps, lead your long suit to try to force declarer to ruff. With the trump suit weakened, declarer may lose control of the hand. *Trump length, lead length.*

## Leading against slams

Against a small slam it often pays to be bold and lead away from a king or queen. Against 6NT or a grand slam your aim is to avoid giving a trick away. Choose the safest possible lead.

# Third-hand play

## The high-low signal

When the opening lead is an honour card, following suit with a high spot-card asks partner to continue the suit. Playing your lowest card asks partner to switch to some other suit. The signal is confirmed on the second round of the suit. High-low (sometimes called an 'echo') is encouraging, a low-high sequence is discouraging.

| PARTNER LEADS | DUMMY DECLARER | | YOUR PLAY AGAINST NT |
|---|---|---|---|
| A K 3 | 9 6 5 | Q 8 7 2 | Play the eight to encourage. You want the suit continued. |
| | J 10 4 | | |
| A K J 3 | 9 6 5 | 10 8 4 | Play the 4 to discourage. The next lead in the suit should come from you. |
| | Q 7 2 | | |
| A K 7 3 | 9 6 5 | Q J 10 4 | Signal with the highest card you can afford. The Q-signal tells partner you have the J. |
| | 8 2 | | |
| Q J 9 6 | 10 4 3 | K 7 2 | Encourage with the seven. You want the suit continued. |
| | A 8 5 | | |
| Q J 9 6 | 10 4 3 | 8 7 2 | Discourage with the 2. It costs a trick if partner leads the suit again. |
| | A K 5 | | |
| J 10 9 6 3 | A Q | 8 7 4 2 | Start an echo when you have four cards in partner's suit. |
| | K 5 | | |

## Reverse signals

In this method, lowest card is encouraging, high discouraging (low-like, high-hate). This style is favoured by strong players.

# Third-hand play *continued*

Similar signals are given in defence against suit contracts, but there are minor differences. Do not echo with four low cards but do echo with a doubleton if you want a ruff.

|  |  |  |
|---|---|---|
| | Q 10 <u>5</u> | Encourage with the four. If partner |
| <u>A</u> K 9 7 3 | 4 2 | partner continues the suit, your |
| | J 8 6 | your 4-then-2 asks for the suit to be |

continued and you can ruff the third round.

## The trump echo

It is standard to play low-high in trumps with two or four trumps and to play high-low with three (or five, if you should be so lucky). Knowing the number of trumps you hold allows partner to work out how many trumps declarer has and also whether you can ruff, perhaps more than once.

## Third-hand high

If dummy has only low cards and partner's lead will not win the trick, third hand plays high. *If the top cards are in sequence, third hand plays the lowest card of the sequence.* You lead top of sequence but third-hand-high plays bottom of sequence.

|  |  |  |
|---|---|---|
| | 8 6 <u>5</u> | Play the ace, otherwise declarer |
| Q J 10 7 3 | <u>A</u> 9 4 2 | will make an undeserved trick. |
| | K | |

|  |  |  |
|---|---|---|
| | 9 6 <u>3</u> | Play the ace. The queen will be |
| K <u>J</u> 10 7 | <u>A</u> 5 4 | trapped when you return the suit. |
| | Q 8 2 | |

|  |  |  |
|---|---|---|
| | 10 6 <u>5</u> | Play the jack. When declarer wins |
| K 8 7 <u>3</u> | Q <u>J</u> 4 | with the ace, partner will know you |
| | A 9 2 | have the queen. Likewise, if you held |

J-10-9-4, the card to play as third-hand-high would be the 9.

*The card played when third hand plays high denies the next lower card.* Thus, the A in third seat denies the K, the K in third seat denies the Q, the Q in third seat denies the J, and so on.

## Third-hand play *continued*

**Exception:** With A-K doubleton in third seat, play the ace first, king second. This indicates the doubleton and partner should give a suit-preference signal on the king to tell you the suit to play next: high card, high suit, low card, low suit (see p. 86).

When dummy has an honour and third seat has a higher honour, if declarer plays low from dummy, tend to keep the higher honour to capture dummy's honour later, particularly if you have dummy's honour almost surrounded.

|  | K 8 5 |  | Encourage with the 9. Partner's Q |
|---|---|---|---|
| Q J 10 7 3 |  | A 9 2 | will win the trick. |
|  | 6 4 |  |  |

|  | Q 8 6 |  | You have dummy's Q surrounded. |
|---|---|---|---|
| 10 9 5 3 |  | K J 4 | The jack will be high enough to |
|  | A 7 2 |  | draw the ace. |

|  | K 7 2 |  | You have the K nearly surrounded. |
|---|---|---|---|
| Q 10 6 3 |  | A J 4 | If partner has the Q, the jack will win. |
|  | 9 8 5 |  | If declarer has the Q, playing the ace gives declarer two tricks. |

|  | A J 5 |  | If you play the Q, declarer can make |
|---|---|---|---|
| K 10 7 3 |  | Q 9 4 | two tricks by finessing the J later. |
|  | 8 6 2 |  | If partner has led from 10-x-x-x, the 9 restricts declarer to two tricks. |

|  | Q 10 8 |  | **Special case:** In a suit contract |
|---|---|---|---|
| J 9 5 3 |  | K 7 4 | partner would not lead from an ace |
|  | A 6 2 |  | and so you should not play the king. Play the 4, discouraging. |

If you put up the king, declarer will make three tricks in all by finessing against partner's jack next time. The same play is correct in a no-trumps contract. Declarer is bound to make a trick even if partner has the ace.

## Third-hand play *continued*

**The rule of eleven:** The lead of the 4$^{th}$-highest card can yield valuable information about the distribution of the suit. A two lead means partner has led from a 4-card suit at most. If a three is led, partner can have four or five cards, but not six.

More can be learned by applying the rule of 11. Subtract the spots on partner's 4$^{th}$-highest lead from 11. The answer is the number of higher cards held by dummy, declarer and third hand. Suppose partner has led a six. $11 - 6 = 5$. If dummy has two cards higher than the 6 and you also have two, declarer has only one card higher than the 6.

|            | K 6 4 |        |
|------------|-------|--------|
| Q 10 8 7   |       | A J 9 3 |
|            | 5 2   |        |

$11 - 7 = 4$. You can see all 4 cards higher than the 7 and know that declarer has none. Play low and let partner keep the lead.

|            | Q 8   |        |
|------------|-------|--------|
| A 10 6 5 3 |       | K 9 7 2 |
|            | J 4   |        |

**Special case:** The rule of 11 tells you declarer has one card higher than the 5. If this were the ace, declarer would have tried the queen

from dummy. Do not finesse against dummy here. Play the king.

**Unblocking:** With a doubleton honour in partner's long suit, play it on the first round of the suit to avoid a blockage.

|          | 8 7 4 |     |
|----------|-------|-----|
| K Q 10 9 3 |     | A 5 |
|          | J 6 2 |     |

Play the ace and return the 5. This is the right play at no-trumps and against a suit contract, too.

|          | 8 6 5 |     |
|----------|-------|-----|
| Q J 10 4 3 |     | K 7 |
|          | A 9 2 |     |

Play the K to get out of partner's way. This is the right play against a suit contract, too.

|          | Q 5   |     |
|----------|-------|-----|
| A 10 9 8 6 3 |   | J 7 |
|          | K 4 2 |     |

Drop the J to avoid blocking the suit. If you retain the jack and lead it later, declarer can play low.

## Third-hand play *continued*

**Returning partner's suit:** Return the higher card when you have only two cards left, but return the original fourth-highest when you began with a 4-card or longer suit.

|  | A J 4 |  |
|---|---|---|
| Q 8 7 3 2 |  | K 10 5 |
|  | 9 6 |  |

When the ten wins, return the king, top of the remaining doubleton. The same applies in a suit contract.

|  | A 9 |  |
|---|---|---|
| K 10 7 4 |  | Q 8 3 2 |
|  | J 6 5 |  |

When the queen wins, return the two, your original fourth-highest. The same applies in a suit contract.

|  | 6 |  |
|---|---|---|
| A J 7 5 4 |  | K 10 9 2 |
|  | Q 8 3 |  |

**Exception:** Play the 10 next. With a high sequence, return the top card to avoid blocking the suit. Likewise, with J-10-x left, return the jack.

|  | 6 |  |
|---|---|---|
| K 10 8 4 3 |  | A J 9 5 2 |
|  | Q 7 |  |

**Exception:** Return the 2. With five cards including the jack, return the fifth-highest. If you return the five, partner may place you with A-5-2 and duck.

**Ducking:** When partner leads your suit against a no-trumps contract it may pay you to play low to maintain communications.

|  | 10 5 3 |  |
|---|---|---|
| 9 6 |  | A K 8 4 2 |
|  | Q J 7 |  |

Lacking an outside entry, encourage with the 8. If partner has an entry, you will make four tricks later.

|  | K 10 9 |  |
|---|---|---|
| 8 2 |  | A Q 7 5 3 |
|  | J 6 4 |  |

Lacking an outside entry, encourage with the 7. If partner has an entry, you will make four tricks later.

|  | A Q |  |
|---|---|---|
| 10 4 |  | K 9 8 7 5 3 |
|  | J 6 2 |  |

Encourage with the nine in order to keep your king for the third round of the suit.

# Second-hand play

The defender in second position should normally play low when a low card is led from dummy or from declarer's hand.

### Declarer leads

|  | K 9 6 2 |  |
|---|---|---|
| J 3 |  | Q 8 5 |
|  | A 10 7 4 |  |

Play the three. If you play the jack, declarer can finesse on the way back to lose no trick in the suit.

|  | Q 7 6 2 |  |
|---|---|---|
| A J 4 |  | 10 5 |
|  | K 9 8 3 |  |

Play the four. If you play the ace or the jack, declarer will lose only one trick in the suit.

|  | J 7 5 4 |  |
|---|---|---|
| Q 8 2 |  | K 9 |
|  | A 10 6 3 |  |

Play low. Otherwise the declarer will make three tricks in the suit.

|  | Q 10 7 3 |  |
|---|---|---|
| A K 5 |  | J 8 4 |
|  | 9 6 2 |  |

Unless you need tricks quickly, play the five. Declarer will probably finesse dummy's ten.

|  | A J 10 6 2 |  |
|---|---|---|
| K 7 3 |  | Q 9 4 |
|  | 8 5 |  |

**Exception:** When dummy has no outside entry, play high in order to kill the suit.

### Dummy leads

|  | K 7 3 |  |
|---|---|---|
| J 9 5 |  | A 8 4 |
|  | Q 10 6 2 |  |

Play low. If you play the ace, it may be your only trick in the suit.

|  | 9 3 |  |
|---|---|---|
| Q 10 8 |  | A 7 6 2 |
|  | K J 5 4 |  |

Play low to give declarer a guess.

|  | K 5 3 |  |
|---|---|---|
| 8 4 |  | Q J 6 |
|  | A 10 9 7 2 |  |

**Exception:** With honour cards in sequence, split the honours to make sure of a trick. Play top of sequence.

## Second-hand play *continued*

**Covering honours:** When an honour card is led from dummy or from declarer's hand, cover with a higher honour if there is a chance of promoting a trick for your side. Covering forces declarer to use two high cards on the one trick and your side may be able to win a later trick with a lower card. Do not cover if doing so helps only declarer. When an honour is led from a sequence, do not cover until the last card of the sequence is played.

### Declarer leads

| | |
|---|---|
| A J 5 3<br>K 10 9     7 6 2<br>Q 8 4 | Cover with the king to promote your ten. Otherwise declarer can make four tricks in the suit. |
| A Q 9 5<br>K 6 2     10 7 3<br>J 8 4 | Cover with the king. This time you must hope that partner has the ten. Play low and declarer has 4 tricks. |
| A Q 10 9<br>K 7 6 3     8 5 2<br>J 4 | Play low, for there is nothing you can promote. Playing the king gives declarer four tricks in the suit. |
| A K 10 6<br>Q 7 3     9 5 4 2<br>J 8 | Cover with the queen and hope that partner has four cards to the nine. |
| A 6 3<br>Q 8 2     K 9 4<br>J 10 7 5 | Play low on the assumption declarer has the ten. If you cover, declarer can make three tricks in the suit. |
| A 7<br>K 6 5 4     8 3 2<br>Q J 10 9 | Play low, for you can expect to score the king on the third round. Play the king and declarer has four tricks. |
| K Q 9 7 4<br>A 3     10 8 5 2<br>J 6 | Play the ace and hope that partner has a second stopper. It is usually right to cover with a doubleton honour. |

## Second-hand play *continued*

A good general rule is to cover when there are two honours on
your left and play low when there are two on your right.

**Dummy leads**

| | | |
|---|---|---|
| | Q J 3 | | Play low on the first lead. If you play |
| 10 7 5 | | K 6 4 | the king, declarer can make 4 tricks |
| | A 9 8 2 | | by running the 9 on the way back. |

QJ3    Play low on the first lead. If you play
10 7 5  K 6 4  the king, declarer can make 4 tricks
A 9 8 2  by running the 9 on the way back.

Q J 3    Cover when you have a doubleton
10 8 5  K 6  (unless declarer has a 7-card suit).
A 9 7 4 2  Otherwise your side makes no trick.

J 7 4    Cover with the queen and hope that
A 9 5  Q 6 2  this will promote partner's cards.
K 10 8 3

10 6 3    Cover with the king. If you play low
Q 8 4  K 9 2  declarer can make 3 tricks. Cover
A J 7 5  and you restrict declarer to two.

J 10 9 7    Play low when an honour card is led
Q 2  K 6 5 3  from a sequence. If you play low,
A 8 4  you restrict declarer to two tricks.

When partner is known to have two cards or fewer in the suit,
it can be costly to cover an honour led from dummy. In the
examples below, declarer is known to have a 6+ suit.

**Dummy leads**

J 9 5    Play low else declarer has no loser.
Q  K 2  To cover would also destroy a trick
A 10 8 7 6 4 3  if partner has the ace singleton.

J 5    Play low and your side scores three
K  Q 10 9 3  tricks. Cover with the queen (very
A 8 7 6 4 2  tempting) and you make only two.

85

## Signals

**Suit-preference signals:** In defence against a suit contract, when you wish to indicate where your entry lies, play your highest card if your entry is in the high suit and your lowest card if your entry is in the low suit.

```
          7 6 4            You lead the K and Q and declarer
K Q J 10 3        5 2      ducks twice. On the third round, play
          A 9 8            the jack for a high suit entry, the 3 for
                           a low suit entry (and the 10 if your
                           entry is in the middle suit).
```

```
  K Q J 9 8                In a suit contract partner leads the 3.
3            A 7 5 4 2      You win with the ace and even though
  10 6                     declarer plays the ten, you know that
                           partner has led a singleton. Return the
```
7 to ask partner to play back the higher suit, return the 2 if you want partner to play back the lower suit (trumps excluded).

Partner pre-empted 3♢ and leads the ♢2 against 4♡. The ♢2 cannot be fourth-highest. It is a suit-preference signal, asking for a club return. It is highly likely that partner is void in clubs.

**High-encouraging discards:** High card encouraging, low card discouraging can be used also for discarding. If so, the discard of a high card asks partner to lead that suit at first opportunity. If you cannot afford to part with a high card, discard low cards in the other two suits. Partner should be able to work it out.

**Reverse discards:** In this method, low cards are encouraging and high cards discouraging. This protects your high cards in a suit.

**Suit-preference discards** (recommended): The suit discarded is not wanted. A high discard asks for the higher of the other suits, a low discard asks for the lower of the other suits.

Suppose spades are trumps. Playing suit-preference discards, what would it mean if partner discards the (a) ♢9? (b) ♡2? (c) ♣3?
(a) ♢9 says, 'Not diamonds. Higher of the others. Play a heart.'
(b) ♡2 says, 'Not hearts. Lower of the other two. Play a club.'
(c) ♣3 says, 'Not clubs. Lower of the others. Play a diamond.'

# Signals *continued*

**Count signals:** When declarer leads a suit from hand or from dummy, either in a trump contract or at no-trumps, it can be helpful for the defenders to indicate their length to each other. To do this, play high-low with an even number of cards and lowest with an odd number. These signals can be especially useful when dummy has a long suit with no outside entry.

```
   K J 10 7 4            Declarer leads the Q. On seeing the 3
8 5 3            A 9 2    East knows South has a doubleton and
   Q 6                   so takes the ace on the second round.
                         Had West played the eight on the
```
first round, East would hold off with the ace until the third round.

**Reverse count signals** (recommended): In this method, you play lowest from an even number and high-low with an odd number. This saves wasting a useful top card from a doubleton.

Whichever method you play, do not give count religiously if doing so may help declarer locate a vital queen, jack or ten.

## Probabilities

This table indicates the probability of each division of the cards in the unseen hands. Such information can be useful.

| MISSING | DIVISION | PROBABILITY | MISSING | DIVISION | PROBABILITY |
|---------|----------|-------------|---------|----------|-------------|
| 2 cards | 1-1 | 52% | 6 cards | 3-3 | 36% |
|         | 2-0 | 48% |         | 4-2 | 48% |
|         |     |     |         | 5-1 | 15% |
| 3 cards | 2-1 | 78% |         | 6-0 | 1% |
|         | 3-0 | 22% |         |     |    |
|         |     |     | 7 cards | 4-3 | 62% |
| 4 cards | 2-2 | 40% |         | 5-2 | 30.5% |
|         | 3-1 | 50% |         | 6-1 | 7% |
|         | 4-0 | 10% |         | 7-0 | 0.5% |
|         |     |     |         |     |    |
| 5 cards | 3-2 | 68% |         |     |    |
|         | 4-1 | 28% |         |     |    |
|         | 5-0 | 4% |         |     |    |

PROBABILITIES

## Probabilities *continued*

It is worth noting that when the opponents have an odd number of cards in a suit the most probable division is an even one. When the opponents have an even number of cards, an even break is not the most likely one. This can be encapsulated:

*Odd numbers break evenly, even numbers break oddly.*

*Another useful memory aid:* What are the odds for a 3-2, 4-1 or 4-2 split? Reverse these numbers for a close approximation. The 3-2 break occurs about 2/3 of the time, the 4-1 break about 1/4 of the time and the 4-2 break about 2/4 or half the time.

A knowledge of the table on page 87 can help to determine the best line of play. It is easily seen, for instance, that a simple finesse (50%) is a better bet than a 3 – 3 break (36%) but a worse prospect than a 3 – 2 break (68%).

**Finesse or drop**

From that table we can also extract information about the probability of an enemy honour card dropping.

| MISSING | PROBABILITY OF AN HONOUR CARD BEING: | | |
|---|---|---|---|
| | SINGLETON | DOUBLETON | TREBLETON |
| 2 cards | 52% | 48% | - - - |
| 3 cards | 26% | 52% | 22% |
| 4 cards | 12% | 40% | 38% |
| 5 cards | 6% | 27% | 41% |
| 6 cards | 2.5% | 16% | 36% |
| 7 cards | 1% | 9% | 27% |

This enables us to form a general rule for finessing:

| MISSING | |
|---|---|
| 2 cards | Play for the drop. |
| 3 or 4 cards | Finesse for the king but not for the queen or jack. |
| 5 or 6 cards | Finesse for the king or queen but not for the jack. |
| 7 cards | Finesse for the king, queen or jack |

# Finessing technique

## When the opponents have two honours

If a suit is missing two honours, say the K and Q, they will be divided between the opponents 52% of the time and in the same hand 48% of time, 24% on your left and 24% on your right. A double finesse therefore has an excellent chance of success. With A-J-10 opposite low cards, you will fail to make two tricks only when the K and Q are both behind the ace, a 24% chance. The probability of making two tricks is 76%.

As a general rule when taking a finesse, lead a low card. Lead a high card for a finesse only if you can afford to expend two honour cards to capture one.

| HOLDING | YOU SHOULD |
|---|---|
| A Q 10 4<br>J 3 2 | Lead the 2 and finesse the 10. If it wins, return to hand and lead the 3 for a finesse of the Q. |
| A K J 4<br>10 3 2 | Lead the 2 to the ace. If the Q has not dropped, return to hand and lead the 3, finessing the jack. |
| K Q J 5<br>4 3 2 | Lead the 2 to the J. If it wins, return to hand and lead the 3 to the Q. Return to hand and lead the 4. |
| Q J 5 4<br>K 3 2 | Lead the 2 and play the jack. If it wins, return to hand and lead the 3 to the queen. |
| Q J 5 4<br>A 3 2 | Cash the ace, lead the 2 and play the J. If it wins, return to hand and lead the 3 to the queen. This gives the best chance of three tricks. |
| A 10 6 5<br>J 4 3 2 | Lead the 2 and finesse the 10. *But*, if you believe that East has a doubleton, lead the jack and run it. |
| K J 5 4<br>10 3 2 | Lead the 2 and finesse the jack. If it wins, return to hand and lead the 3. |
| A J 10 2<br>Q 9 3 | Run the 9 first, then the queen. The lead thus remains in your hand for a third finesse. |
| A J 10 8<br>9 3 2 | Lead the 2 and finesse the ten. Subsequently run the 9, retaining the lead in hand for a third finesse. |

# Finessing technique *continued*

| HOLDING | YOU SHOULD |
| --- | --- |
| A Q 9<br>4 3 2 | Lead the 2 and finesse the 9 in case West has J-10-x(-x). Later lead the 3 and finesse the Q. |
| A J 9<br>4 3 2 | Lead the 2 and finesse the 9. If this draws the king or queen, later lead the 3 and finesse the jack. |
| K 10 9<br>4 3 2 | Lead the 2 and finesse the 9. Subsequently lead the 3 and finesse the ten. |
| Q 4 3<br>K 10 2 | Lead the 2 and play the queen. When possible, lead the 3 from dummy later and finesse the ten. |
| J 4 3<br>Q 9 2 | Lead the 2 and play the jack. Later lead the 3 and finesse the 9. |
| Q 7 5 3<br>K 6 4 2 | Lead low from either hand and play the honour. If this wins, play low from both hands next time. If |

you can tell which opponent is likely to have the ace, make the first low card lead from the hand to the right of that opponent so that the player with, hopefully, A-x plays second to the trick.

## The duck

When short of entries, maintain communications by conceding the first round of a suit. The duck is most useful at no-trumps. For the following examples, dummy has no outside entry:

| HOLDING | YOU SHOULD |
| --- | --- |
| A K 8 7 5 3<br>4 2 | Play low from both hands on the first round if you need more than two tricks from the suit. |
| A Q 8 7 5 3<br>4 2 | Again play low from both hands on the first round. Finesse the queen on the second round. |
| A K Q 6 4<br>3 2 | Duck on the first round if you need four tricks from this suit. The likely division is 4-2. |
| A 8 7 5 3<br>6 4 2 | This time you must duck twice, keeping the ace for the third round of the suit. |
| A 6 4 2<br>K 5 3 | Duck on the first round or play the K and duck the second round, keeping the A for the third round. |

# The hold-up

When the opponents attack your weak spot at no-trumps, refuse to take your high cards at once ('hold up') to sever communications between the defenders' hands.

**West leads**                    AT NO-TRUMPS

|  | 7 6 |  | Hold up your A until the third round. |
| K J 9 5 3 |  | Q 8 4 | If the suit breaks 5-3, perhaps West |
|  | A 10 2 |  | has no outside entry. |

|  | 7 6 4 |  | Hold up your A for one round to |
| Q J 10 8 2 |  | K 3 | guard against the 5-2 division. |
|  | A 9 5 |  |  |

|  | 7 4 |  | Difficult. If you can keep East off |
| A J 9 6 5 2 |  | 10 3 | lead, win trick 1. If you can keep |
|  | K Q 8 |  | West off lead but not East, duck |
|  |  |  | trick 1 and hope the suit splits 6-2. |

|  | 7 6 4 |  | If West has the outside entry, win |
| A 10 8 3 2 |  | Q 5 | trick 1. If you cannot keep East off |
|  | K J 9 |  | lead, play the 9. |

|  | 7 6 2 |  | Hold up with two stoppers when |
| Q 10 8 5 4 |  | J 3 | you must lose the lead twice in |
|  | A K 9 |  | in developing your tricks. |

# Blocking

Certain holdings allow you to block the run of the enemy suit.

**West leads**                    AT NO-TRUMPS

|  | A J 5 |  | To guard against a 5-2 split, play the |
| Q 10 9 6 4 |  | K 3 | ace and knock out West's entry before |
|  | 8 7 2 |  | the suit can be unblocked. |

|  | A 7 5 |  | Play the ace if you expect West to |
| Q 10 9 6 4 |  | K 3 | have the outside entry. With no |
|  | J 8 2 |  | entry, it does East no good to unblock. |

## Blocking *continued*

**West leads**

AT NO-TRUMPS

A 6

K J 8 5 3        Q 7

10 9 4 2

Play the ace and attack West's entry while the suit is still blocked.

K 10 4

9 5        A J 8 7 3

Q 6 2

Play the king. If East ducks you make two tricks. If East takes the ace, the suit cannot be continued without giving you two tricks.

## Unblocking

You can unblock your own intermediates and high cards to provide entries where they are most needed.

**West leads**

J 10 4

K 9 6 5 3        A 7

Q 8 2

Needing an entry to dummy, play the jack (in case West has the A-K) and drop the queen under the ace.

A 10 7 2

K 9 8 3        Q 6 5

J 4

Drop the jack under the queen to prepare for a later finesse of the ten.

A Q 9

J 10 8 7 3        6 2

K 5 4

Needing three entries to dummy, drop the king under the ace and later finesse the 9.

**Declarer leads**

K 9 4

10        J 7 6 2

A Q 8 5 3

Play the ace and unblock the 9. Play low card to the king and you can pick up the rest by finessing the 8.

Q 8 3

9        K 10 6 5

A J 7 4 2

Lead the 8, unblocking, for a finesse of the J. When West drops the 9 (or 10) return a low card to the Q. If East takes the king, you can finesse the 7 later.

# Precautionary plays

These are plays that cost nothing and are merely a matter of playing the cards in the right order to guard against a bad break.

| HOLDING | YOU SHOULD |
|---|---|
| K Q 9 3<br>A 10 5 4 2 | Missing J-x-x-x, keep a top honour in each hand. Lead low to the K or Q to make sure of 5 tricks. If either defender shows out, the finesse is marked. |
| K Q 9 3<br>A 8 5 4 2 | Missing J-10-x-x, keep two honours together. Cash the ace to ensure 5 tricks when East is void. Nothing can be done if West is void. |
| Q 6 5 3<br>K J 8 4 2 | Missing A-10-9-x, keep two honour together. Lead low to the Q first to cater for a void with West. If East is void, you always lose two tricks. |
| J 5 4 3 2<br>A Q 9 7 6 | Lead the jack from dummy to make sure of 5 tricks when West is void. |
| A<br>J 10 6 5 4 2 | Cash the ace, return to hand lead a low card. You will make four tricks when the suit breaks 3 – 3 and when either defender has a doubleton honour. |
| 9 4 3<br>A K 10 5 2 | Cash the ace, then lead the 2 to cater for Q-J-x-x with East. |
| J 3<br>A Q 6 5 4 2 | Cash the ace first in order to guard against a singleton king. |

## Safety plays

A safety play is a means of guarding against a bad break where you give up a trick, perhaps unnecessarily, in order to reduce the risk of losing two tricks. The trick lost represents the premium of the insurance policy.

| 8 6 4 2<br>A Q 7 5 3 | For the best chance of four tricks, cash the ace, cross to dummy and lead towards the queen. This guards against singleton king with West. |
|---|---|
| 6 4 3<br>A Q J 5 2 | For four tricks, in case West has K-singleton, cash the ace, enter dummy and lead towards the Q-J. |

## Safety plays *continued*

| HOLDING | YOU SHOULD |
|---|---|
| 2<br>K Q 7 6 5 4 3 | Lead the 2. If you can afford two losers, play low from hand to guard against singleton A with West. |
| A K 4<br>9 8 7 6 5 2 | Lead the 2 and finesse the 4 if West plays the 3. This ensures five tricks if West has Q-J-10-3. |
| J 2<br>A K 9 6 5 4 3 | Lead low from hand to make sure of six tricks against any distribution. |
| 10 4 3<br>A K 8 5 2 | Cash the ace. If an honour drops on either side or West plays the 9, continue with the 2 to make sure of four tricks. |
| Q 7 4 2<br>A J 8 5 3 | Needing four tricks, lead the queen from dummy to cater for K-10-9-6 with East. |
| A 9 3<br>K J 5 4 2 | If you can afford a loser, cash the K and continue with the 2, playing the 9 if West plays low. This guarantees 4 tricks unless the suit breaks 5-0. |
| A J 4 3<br>K 9 5 2 | To make sure of three tricks, cash the ace and lead the 3, inserting the 9 if East plays low. |
| A 5 3<br>K J 4 2 | For the best chance to score three tricks, cash the king and the ace, then lead towards the jack. |
| A J 4 3<br>10 6 5 2 | To make certain of two tricks, cash the ace and continue with the 3. |
| K 6 4 3<br>Q 7 5 2 | For the best chance for just two tricks, play low both hands to guard against a singleton ace. |
| Q 10 4 3<br>K 5 2 | For the best chance for two tricks, lead low from either hand to the K or Q. If this loses, cash the other top honour before leading from hand towards the ten. |
| Q 10 7 5 3<br>A 9 6 4 2 | To guarantee four tricks, including a chance for all five, lead low from dummy and insert the 9 if East plays low. Caters for K-J-8 in either hand and scores 5 tricks if East has the singleton king. |

## The play from dummy at trick one

In each of the layouts below, North leads the 3. What should you play from dummy (1) at no-trumps? (2) in a suit contract?

| YOUR HAND | DUMMY HOLDS | YOUR BEST PLAY IS: |
|---|---|---|
| 9 5 4 | K 6 | (1) Play the K. Your best chance for 1 trick.<br>(2) Play low if North would not lead a low card away from the ace. |
| J 5 4 | K 6 | (1) and (2) Play low to guarantee one trick. |
| J 4 | K 6 | (1) Play low. It is a guess but you may as well play low and hope North has the queen.<br>(2) Play low. South should have the ace. |
| Q 5 4 | K 6 | (1) Play the K. If this wins, your Q-x is still a stopper against North.<br>(2) Play low. South should have the ace and may err by playing it. |
| Q 10 4 | K 6 | (1) and (2) Play low to ensure two tricks. |
| A 10 4 | K 6 | (1) and (2) Play low. You have two tricks already and will score a third if North has led from a suit headed by the Q-J. |

*Rule 1: If dummy has an honour and declarer has the 10 and a higher non-touching honour (A-10, K-10, Q-10), play low from dummy and let the lead come to your honour-10. This either guarantees, or is your best chance for, an extra trick.*

*Rule 2: If it is correct to play low from dummy with honour-doubleton, it is correct to play low from dummy when dummy has honour to three or longer.*

| A J 4 | K 6 | (1) and (2) Play low to guarantee 3 tricks. |
|---|---|---|
| Q 4 | K 6 2 | (1) and (2) Play low from dummy. |
| 10 5 4 | K J 6 | (1) and (2) Play low from dummy. |

# The play from dummy at trick one *continued*

In each of the layouts below, North leads the 3. What should you play from dummy (1) at no-trumps? (2) in a suit contract?

| YOUR HAND | DUMMY HOLDS | YOUR BEST PLAY IS: |
|---|---|---|
| A 9 4 | K 10 5 | (1) and (2) Play low from dummy. |
| A 8 4 | K 10 5 | (1) and (2) Play low from dummy. |
| A 4 | Q 5 | (1) and (2) Play the queen. |
| A 6 4 | Q 5 | (1) and (2) Play the queen. |
| A 10 4 | Q 5 | (1) and (2) Play low for 2 tricks. Rule 1. |
| K 4 | Q 10 5 | (1) and (2) Play the 10. This yields 2 tricks if North has the jack or the ace. |
| A 4 | Q 10 5 | (1) and (2) Play the 10. Similar to the above. |
| A J 4 | Q 9 5 | (1) and (2) Play the 9. Best hope for 3 tricks. |
| J 5 4 | Q 6 | (1) and (2)  Play low to ensure one trick. |
| A K 4 | J 5 | (1) and (2) Play the jack. |
| A 6 4 | J 5 | (1) and (2) Play the jack. |
| A 10 4 | J 5 | (1) and (2) Play low for 2 tricks. Rule 1. |
| A 5 4 | J 9 6 | (1) and (2) Play the 9. Best hope for 2 tricks. |
| 6 5 4 | A J 9 | (1) and (2) Play the 9. Best hope for 2 tricks. |
| A 9 4 | J 6 5 | (1) and (2) Play low. Best hope for 2 tricks. |
| 9 5 4 | A J 6 | (1) and (2) Play low. Best hope for 2 tricks. |
| K 9 4 | A J 6 | (1) and (2) Play low. Best hope for 3 tricks. |

*Note: In the above five examples, the focus is on the 9 each time.*

| A K 4 | 10 5 | (1) and (2) Play the 10. |
|---|---|---|
| K Q 4 | 10 5 | (1) and (2) Play the 10. |